International Journal of the Sociology of Language

JOSHUA A. FISHMAN

General Editor

8

Language and Education in the Third World

EDITED BY JACK BERRY

1976

MOUTON

THE HAGUE · PARIS

Subscription information

One year subscription covers four issues:

Institutions, libraries:	80 Dutch guilders	$31	£16	145 F	80 DM
Individuals, PREPAID:	50 Dutch guilders	$19.50	£10	91 F	50 DM

The Dutch guilder price is definitive

Payment can be made by cheque, bankdraft, moneyorder or Unesco coupons and should accompany orders to ensure rapid handling.

Subscription at regular rate, single or back issues may be ordered through any bookseller or subscription agent, or directly from the publishers, Mouton & Co.

Subscription orders for Latin America (including Mexico) may be placed with Swets and Zeitlinger, Caixa postal 18.026 – Meier, 20.000 Rio de Janeiro, Brazil, or Swets and Zeitlinger, Casilla correo 10.249 – Katalenic, Lima, Peru.

Individuals may subscribe at the reduced rate for private use only and exclusively with the publishers at the addresses in the Netherlands or France. Orders at reduced rates will not be billed.
DELIVERY WILL ONLY BE MADE ON RECEIPT OF PAYMENT.

Netherlands
Mouton
P.O.B. 482
NL-2076 The Hague

France
Mouton
7, Rue Dupuytren
F-75006 Paris

The contents of this issue are identical to the contents of Linguistics 175

ISBN 90 279 7851 4
© 1976, Mouton & Co. The Hague, the Netherlands
Photoset in Malta by Interprint (Malta) Ltd
Printed in the Netherlands by Intercontinental Graphics

Table of Contents

Introduction

[handwritten: Is aspiration part of identity? Acheiving of maintaining a social identity - via education + employment]

The contributions sociolinguistic theory can make to a better understanding of language and language-related problems in education has long been recognized. In this issue of *IJSL* will be found five papers which discuss in sociolinguistic terms various aspects of Language and Education in the Third World. Ruqaia Hasan describes and seeks to explain the loss of "identity" that can be suffered in cross-cultural education, more specifically by students from the Indian sub-continent at English universities. Two papers, Winford and Moses *et al.*, discuss teachers' attitudes to their pupils' speech. And in more general terms, three papers consider creole-standard situations in the Caribbean: Craig, Winford, and Carrington. These three papers, one of them rather long, may seem to give an emphasis to creole language problems in this issue. The emphasis, though quite fortuitous, may not be inappropriate. The language problems in education in creole-standard situations are among the most recalcitrant today and they offer a challenge to both sociolinguists and educationists alike.

JACK BERRY

[handwritten: what effects would we have on identity in a low acheiving compared to a private high acheiving school? standards, expectations, parental acheivment + experience, socialised to accept values + their identity. Meritocracy Aspire]

RUQAIYA HASAN

Socialization and Cross-Cultural Education

The aim of this paper is to explore the relationship between socialization and cross-cultural education, with specific reference to the Indo-Pakistani subcontinent and England. There is a difficulty in talking of the global culture of a whole community: it necessarily implies ignoring subcultural differences, which are important. Although this restricts the discussion to a general level, such general discussion may be justifiable on the assumption that the subcultures of a given culture are closely related to each other at least at some level of analysis. The culture of the Chinese Muslim community might differ in some respects from other Chinese subcultures; nonetheless, it is closer to the global Chinese culture than it is to the culture of the Indo-Pakistani Muslim community, which in its turn is more readily relatable to the subcontinental culture as a whole than to the Arab or Turkish or Egyptian culture.

By "cross-cultural education" I refer primarily to the situation where an individual from culture A typically migrates temporarily, to culture B, in order to acquire some academic qualification. Undoubtedly, the term is capable of a much wider interpretation: it could, for instance, be employed to refer to the situation, common in ex-colonies, where the contents of knowledge originating from and specific to the colonizing cultures are included within the curriculum. However, the problems that may arise from this latter situation differ qualitatively from those specific to the former. So, the Indo-Pakistani student, learning, say, Newtonian Physics in some Indo-Pakistani institution is, in a very real sense, not exposed to a set of problems which this same student faces when learning the same body of material once he is a student at a British university. The cultural origin and identity of the content of knowledge, although important, would appear to be not as important in this situation as the symbolic factors inherent in the culturally different systems of education.

It is quite obvious that moving from one culture to another would involve greater or lesser problems of personal adjustment, e.g., in food habits, physical living conditions, and in day-to-day interaction with other humans. Relevant as these problems are to the total well-being of the foreign student, I am not concerned here with these, as they appear to me to impinge only indirectly upon the main problem of the successful completion of the educational process itself. Rather, I would like to concentrate upon those factors which, most probably, directly affect the foreign student's educational achievements.

In looking at these, I would like to make a distinction between those factors which relate to the mechanics of the educational process and those which relate to the social meanings of the educational system. Both in the formulation of the problems facing a foreign student and in the remedies sought for resolving them, it would appear, that more attention is paid to the former type – the ones that relate to the mechanics of the educational process. So, for example, the problems and remedies tend to centre round the "medium" of education or the explicit "content" of knowledge to be transmitted. In effect, then, we ask: (a) does the foreign student have sufficient mastery of the language through which knowledge is transmitted? and, (b) does the foreign student understand – or, is he at that state of readiness where he could be expected to understand – the subject matter of what he is about to be taught? The statement of requirements formulated in terms of prior knowledge which permit the admission of a foreign student to a specific course can be seen as an effort to cope with the problems arising from content. On the other hand, dilemmas arise from the fact that medium and content are inextricably intertwined. This is especially the case in the domain of social sciences and human letters, for here, every element of content is typically transmitted solely verbally, and evaluation of the student's achievement is based upon his verbal presentation of knowledge, which through this verbal presentation becomes available for examination.

The big boom in the business of teaching English as a foreign language is an off-shoot of the mechanical problems in cross-cultural education. Because of this inevitably close relationship between the medium and the content, once the hurdle of admission has been successfully passed, the formulation of the problems and their solutions tend to centre round the question of medium. Nor can this emphasis be brushed aside lightly; there can be no doubt that both the sufficient mastery of medium and the readiness to absorb the concepts relevant to a content are necessary conditions for educational success. Nonetheless, at least three considerations deserve attention here. First, although groups of foreign students with different degrees of mastery of English arrive at the English universities every year, it is yet to be demonstrated that there is a clear causal correlation between the educational success of the group and the extent of its knowledge of English. Thus, I doubt if it is true, that more Turkish or Thai students fail at English universities than do the Indo-Pakistani ones, though there is good reason to believe that due to historical accidents the latter may be credited with possessing "better English". Secondly, although in the context of cross-cultural education, the problem of medium and content may possess certain characteristics specific to it, it is still true that this problem is one which has to be considered with reference to the native student as well. In most educational systems, the purpose of examination is to function as a traffic control sign: if you pass, then the light is green and it allows you to proceed – in other words you are judged ready to cope with the medium and content of the next demarcated stage. Because the staging is largely continuous within one educational system, we tend to assume that the problems of medium and content-readiness are automatically solved by the examination system. However, this assumption is not always proved correct as can be seen most clearly at the stages of transition from primary to secondary and from secondary to university education in England. Third, and last, the emphasis on the mechanical aspects of cross-cultural education has had the effect of pushing into the background some problems of a different kind, which are at least as serious, if not more so. These are the problems that relate to the social meanings of the educational systems.

Some reasons may be suggested for this preoccupation with the mechanical aspects of cross-cultural education. It is clear that the problems arising here are tangible, for which some kind of solution appears to be available without any change in the social meanings of the educational systems; they are for the most part problems of the type that the educational institutions have to cope with, as a matter of course, in the education of the native students. No matter how vague the concepts behind "sufficient mastery of the medium" and "state of readiness for the content of knowledge" may be, it is to be assumed that some measurement of both is feasible, while remaining within the established evaluative framework. Equally, no matter what the difficulties inherent in the successful teaching of medium or in increasing the conceptual ability of the student, the explicit practices of the educational institutions rest on the assumption that both goals can be achieved. The success of the modes of coping with these problems can also be assessed by remaining within the educational framework. Further, despite the close interdependence between medium and content, the two can be dissociated to some extent, as in the practice of those university teachers who ignore grammatical mistakes, inept lexical selections, misspellings, and the like, so long as the content of the student's offering is intelligible. For obvious reasons, such dissociation is easier in the "hard sciences", especially where the content involves statements of formuli or is based upon practical experiments. It is this dissociation that lends these problems their tangible shape and encourages the belief that the two can be tackled separately in their separate contexts, the sum of the practices leading to a successful solution at the end of the process. All in all, then, this is an area in which one knows – or at least one assumes one knows – where one is; one knows also what is to be done and one knows to what extent the doing is successful. By contrast, those problems in cross-cultural education which arise as a result of the differences in the social meanings of the educational systems belonging to two distinct cultures are much more intangible, especially since it is by no means certain that those involved in the educational process have an explicit realization of these meanings. Moreover, at least at the moment, there appears very little that can be done to solve these problems, while still remaining within the established framework of the educational institutions. Here, not only do we not know where we are but we also lack ideas as to what can be done or how the success of the doing is to be assessed.

The question arises as to what one means by talking about the "social meanings of the educational systems". Is this some more technical jargon to refer to the fact that educational processes vary in some visible, manifest ways from one society to another? I would suggest that this is not the case. It is obvious that there are manifest differences in the educational processes across cultures, for example, in the size of the class, the allocation of time to certain subjects, the pedagogical practices and modes, and criteria for evaluation. These manifest differences meet the eye, as the audible noise of language produced meets the ear. But just as in language there is more than meets the ear, so also in the educational process there is more than meets the eye: in both cases the manifest is representationally related to something which underlies the manifest; the motivating force for both is to be sought at the level of meaning. Without pressing the analogy too far, the manifest level in both cases can be studied systematically and accurately only if it is related to the level that Hsu (1971a) has called the level of "content", i.e., the social meaning. I shall avoid using Hsu's term "content" in this article for fear that it may be confused with content in "content of knowledge", but I hope the point is clear that essentially the analysis of a social institution is no less a "quest for meaning" than the analysis of language is (Whorf 1956; Firth 1957).

A newcomer to the field of sociology and anthropology is struck by the fact that often a particular social institution is isolated for intensive study, but, just as often, little or no effort is made to relate the analysis to the society as a whole. In such analyses, each institution can be seen as having a set of functions and a specific structural shape, but the question of how and at what level of abstraction one such institution can be related to others is seldom explored in any detail. Such atomic studies of social institutions are, of course, interesting in their own right, but it could not be claimed that they contribute materially towards the statement of any principles which account for the coherence of a society or its culture. In a series of thought-provoking writings, Hsu (1963, 1971a, 1971b) has criticized the practice of analyzing the kinship system as a self-sufficient whole with little regard to how it relates to the rest of the culture, while Douglas has shown (1972) that manifestly varied social phenomena can be seen as governed by one single abstract principle. The rationale for approaching the study of social institutions in this integrative manner is to be found in the very nature and definition of culture. If culture is a "design for living" (Kluckhohn 1945), it would seem to follow that the individual elements of the design must be related to each other in some specific ways. The principles contributing to the unity of the design are likely to be pervasive, so that at the deepest level of analysis a largely homogeneous set of principles may be found to run through the diverse social institutions, like a strain running through a musical composition.

It may be instructive at this point to turn to Whorf's hypotheses, as these are with specific reference to a very much more easily delimited symbolic system than that of culture. As I see it, Whorf was not concerned with the individual elements in the total inventory of the atoms of meaning available to human languages; rather, his primary concern was with characteristic modes of meaning. In linguistics, Whorf stands out as an exception in that he concentrated on the organizational principles at the semantic level, rather than on the atomic semantic components themselves. This is what explains the necessity for his emphatically repeated statements that the characteristic mode of meaning cannot be studied by looking at individual encoding devices, be they paradigms, single lexical items, a syntactic category or any one syntactic system of agnates. Attempts at testing Whorf's hypothesis by reference to any isolated patterns of the latter type (Brown and Lenneberg 1954; Fishman 1972), whatever they may prove or disprove, still remain irrelevant to this essential part of the Whorfian hypothesis, namely that, the universe of meaning for each language is organized along certain dominant principles, which pervade many patterns of distinct morphological types. What Whorf tried to do with reference to language is what, it appears to me, scholars such as Hsu, Douglas, and Bernstein, to mention but three, are attempting to do in the domain of the nonverbal meanings – that is, if I am not mistaken in my interpretation of these writers. The gist of what has been said above may be summed up in one sentence as follows: a given culture is essentially a symbolic system where every element holds together. It may well be true that in the symbolic system, *culture*, this characteristic is less pronounced than it is in the symbolic system, *language*; nonetheless, culture is not a conglomerate of isolated institutions bearing only accidental, spatial or practical-functional relationships to each other (Hoijer, 1948). Whatever else may or may not be true of culture universally, this certainly seems to be true: there is method in the madness of every culture. The apparently irreconcilable aspects of a culture may not necessarily prove the absence of method; they may only be indicative of an analysis that needs to be carried further in depth.

From the above point of view, then, it would follow that, at the deepest level of analysis, the social institution of education must be seen to be related to the total design of living in a society. In short, it can be seen as an expression of some dominant principles within the given culture. For the purposes of this paper, I shall closely follow (my own interpretation of) Bernstein's hypotheses regarding the symbolic relationship between the educational system and the society in which it is embedded. In his "Classification and framing of educational knowledge" (1971a), Bernstein concentrates on two aspects of education: the curriculum and the pedagogy. "In all educational institutions there is a formal punctuation of time into periods" (p. 203); each period is set aside for some given "content" and we can examine this aspect according to whether the boundary between one content and another is "clear cut or blurred" (p. 204). When the boundary is clear cut, there is a "closed" relationship between the contents; when the boundary between contents is relatively open or blurred, the relationship between the contents is "open". By reference to these two relationships, Bernstein sets up two types of curriculum: (i) the collection type, where the relationship between the contents is closed and the boundary between contents is clear cut and (ii) the integrated type, where the relationship between the contents is open and the boundary between them is blurred. The classification of knowledge is said to be "strong" in the first type, and "weak" in the second. Thus the classification of knowledge makes contact with curriculum and content.

By contrast, the frame of educational knowledge makes contact with pedagogy. "Frame refers to the range of options available to the teacher and taught in the *control* of what is transmitted and received in the context of the pedagogical relationship. Strong framing entails reduced options; weak framing entails a range of options. Thus frame refers to the degree of control teacher and pupil possess over the selection, organization and pacing of knowledge transmitted and received in the pedagogical relationship" (pp. 205–6). Questions regarding framing can be, then, examined at least from two angles: the degree of discretion allowed to the student by the teacher in the pedagogical relationship and the degree of discretion allowed to the teacher by the boundary maintainers. Where both the classification and framing of educational knowledge is strong, typically a hierarchical relationship is built up in which while the student has less discretion vis-à-vis the teacher, the teacher himself has reduced discretion vis-à-vis the boundary maintainers. In such an educational system, if the student is not free to control the selection, organization, and pacing of knowledge to be received, then it is equally true that the teacher himself is largely not free in what to teach over what period. Perhaps, it would be pertinent to add that the greater the centralization of control, the more likely it is that constraints will be imposed both on the teacher and the taught.

The actual classification and framing of educational knowledge in any given culture is not likely to run anomalous to the culture as a whole. Although several dominant cultural principles or mores might operate simultaneously to determine the actual shape of the educational system in these respects, some generalizations can still be made about the relationship of a culture and the type of classification and framing to be found within the educational system. It is thus that I interpret Bernstein's comment: "where classification is strong, the boundaries between the different contents . . . sharply drawn . . . it presupposes strong boundary maintainers" (p. 206). One of the functions of clear-cut, unblurred boundaries is to create "a strong sense of membership and so a specific identity" (p. 206). If this type of analysis is applied to the Indo-Pakistani educational system, we would find that the predictions above are more than fulfilled.

Whatever the diversity of the subcontinental culture, scholars are agreed at least about one attribute, which I regard as a dominant principle having a pervasive effect on phenomena of varied manifest shapes. The subcontinental culture is a culture which jealously guards the ascribed, communal boundaries between segregates. So, the boundaries may be those of caste, or they may be determined by sex or they may be determined by age, kinship relation or by occupation. The one thing that is in common to all such boundaries is that they are regarded – or, it may be more accurate to say that they are affectively reacted to, rather than explicitly or intellectually analysed as – sacrosanct and irrevocable. In the classification of educational knowledge, the typical pattern is that of "collection-type curriculum". The contents of the curriculum are well-insulated from each other. Nor does this tendency show any significant variation along the spectrum of the various recognized stages in the educational process; this is the type of curriculum which continues from primary through secondary to the university level. So, at the university level, for graduate courses, there are well established content-constellations that can be picked up as a package by a graduating student. Any effort to choose three subjects (contents) of one each from three distinct constellations (which would naturally make up the required number three for a graduating course) will be more often frustrated than not. The boundary is, of course, strongest between those contents which are classified under the general label of physical sciences and those which are relegated to social sciences and fine arts. I would be surprised if there was a single university on the subcontinent where the combination chemistry, art history and painting would be allowed as a legitimate one, though, *a priori*, this combination makes as good sense as English literature, education and philosophy – one of the pre-packaged course-constellations allowed at most universities in the north. At the level of practice, of course, it is often the timetable that is blamed, but is there any need to point out that unlike mountains, timetables do not possess a *sui generis* existence? They are only cultural artefacts; as such they are governed by the dominant principles of the culture, which same principles partially or wholly control other cultural artefacts also with possibly very different manifest shapes.

I should hasten to add that I am not implying that the Indo-Pakistani educational system is the only one, or even one amongst a few, to possess collection-type curriculum. The strength and weakness of the classification of knowledge is quite obviously relative. In comparing the English educational system with those of the U.S. and Europe, Bernstein finds the former to possess the strongest classification; but I have no doubt that when the English classification of knowledge is compared with the subcontinental one, the former would appear much weaker than the latter.

I turn now to the element of the framing of knowledge. "Strong frames reduce the power of the pupil over what, when and how he receives knowledge and increase the teacher's power in the pedagogical relationship" (p. 206). It is, perhaps, not too fanciful to suggest that the ancient subcontinental concept of the "guru" epitomizes just such a relationship. Commenting on the relationship of the guru and his disciple, our historical antecedents of the teacher and the taught, Hsu (1963) has remarked on the "affect" that accumulates round this relationship. To Hsu this relationship appears to be characterized by such strong affective ties, that he is inclined to believe it may be stronger than any associated with any kinship dyad in the culture. One may disagree with Hsu's rating of the dyads of relationships – and certainly evidence could be found in the behaviour of the present day generation of members, especially those belonging to the middle-class families, that would throw doubt upon Hsu's hypothesis – yet there appears to be no doubt that taken in their specific contexts, even today, the two dyads – parent-child and teacher-pupil – present close replicas of each other, so that the characteristics of the parent-child dyad in the familial context bears close resemblances to the teacher-pupil dyad in the educational context. A father remains a father, to whom one ideally owes respect and obedience, irrespective of how much authority one's own achieved status might have invested one with in other spheres of life; a teacher remains a teacher, to whom one ideally owes respect and obedience, irrespective of how much one's own knowledge might have outstripped the teacher's knowledge. However, it is pertinent to point out here that although the ancient guru-disciple relationship can be taken as the historical antecedent of the present day teacher-pupil relationship, there are some significant differences between the two. The ancient guru was in a very privileged position: he maintained total control over when, how and what knowledge should be transmitted to his disciples; in addition, unlike the modern teacher, he himself was not subject to control by any external authority whatsoever. There are scores of ancient tales in the culture to substantiate the point that the authority of the guru in the domain of the transmission of knowledge was absolute – there were no external constraints on it, much less any challenge. I believe that I am right in saying that two important factors contributing to this highly privileged position of the guru were the comparatively weak boundary between religion and education and the absence of centralized control over the process of education.

Looking at the present day subcontinental educational system, we would find several manifest characteristics which all point to the exceptionally strong framing of knowledge. Inasmuch as there is a strong centralized control of the educational process today, this has had the effect that the teacher of today does not possess as much discretion vis-à-vis authorities as the guru did. However, within those limits imposed upon the teacher by strong classification and centralization of control, the teacher possesses a great deal of discretion vis-à-vis a student. Not only does the teacher decide what is to be learnt when and how, but his word is also the final one within the domain of his content. Typically, at no stage, within the educational process is the possibility granted that a student may question, much less disagree, with the teacher's views. Thus even in the learning of so-called creative arts, a teacher is likely to insist on the careful imitation of a model provided by him, rather than allow the student to explore on his own. Again the character of this control does not change much with the different stages in the educational process; the practice can be as common at the university level as it is at the primary level. If the beginner is expected to draw from the models perhaps drawn by the teacher himself, the middle-stage student draws from "model-books" provided by the teacher; and even at the university level, the teacher of painting will insist upon certain conventions – in pigment, in contours – which must be followed unvaryingly by all his students. There certainly are exceptions, at the university level, especially; but the exceptions only highlight the norm – they cannot be used for the general characterization of the system as such.

This is clearly a relationship which typically restricts exploration, initiative, and independence; it emphasizes a largely unquestioning acceptance by placing a higher premium on conformity. Another interesting phenomenon is the absence of any kind of explicit or implicit grouping within a class. It is normally recognized that groups of students vary according to how much interest they have in certain contents as opposed to others, as, also, they vary according to how much ability or adaptability they possess in one area as opposed to another. Such grouping naturally implies taking the students as the point of departure and this would not appear to be in agreement with the total pattern of the pedagogical relationship. Hence, streaming, whatever its faults and virtues, has never appeared as an important factor in the subcontinental educational system. If we accept Bernstein's hypothesis that "the stronger the classification and framing of knowledge, the more the educational knowledge tends to be hierarchical and ritualized, the student seen as ignorant, with little status and few rights" (p. 214), then the Indo-Pakistani educational system would be an example par excellence of such phenomena. Another aspect of framing also appears to be relevant to our discussion. Bernstein refers to educational knowledge as "*uncommon-sense knowledge* ... freed from the particular and the local*", while he refers to the "everyday community knowledge of the pupil, his family and peer group" as *common sense knowledge* (p. 215). We can ask then: how strong is the framing of educational knowledge in relation to experiential, community-based, non-school knowledge? How much of the outside can be brought into the class in the context of the pedagogical relationship? Typically, where both the classification and framing of educational knowledge are strong, this also implies a clear cut boundary between the uncommon sense knowledge of the school and the everyday community-based knowledge of the teacher and the taught. "Such insulation creates areas of privacy. For, inasmuch as the community-based experience is irrelevant to the pedagogical frame, those aspects of the self informed by such experiences are also irrelevant. These areas of privacy reduce the penetration of the socializing process, for it is possible to distance oneself from it" (p. 222). That such strong framing of knowledge exists in the Indo-Pakistani educational system will become apparent at once to anyone who cares to examine it. Later, I shall attempt to relate the consequences of such framing to the problems that arise in cross-cultural education.

When the analysis of the Indo-Pakistani educational system is presented thus – and it must be emphasized that the above account is not exhaustive – many would be inclined to conclude that here is a restrictive, narrow, or inefficient system, having very little to recommend it. Such evaluations appear to me to be beside the point. My purpose in making this admittedly limited presentation is not to evaluate the system; I am concerned rather with the question of how it agrees or disagrees with some dominant principles within the culture. To this end, we might profitably take a look at another agency of socialization: the family. In approaching the analysis from this angle, a fact that forces itself upon one's attention is how closely the symbolic meanings of the educational system correspond to those of socialization in the family. As patterns of socialization vary radically from class to class – class being defined by reference to caste and/or economic status and/or the educational status of the parents – I shall concentrate mainly on the patterns of socialization in middle-class families. Such families seldom belong to the lowest castes. Typically, especially in the urban areas, the male parent in these families has had the benefit of formal education up to, at least, a first university degree; the mother would normally be literate though she may not possess a university degree and, in some cases, may not have been exposed to formal education – this is less likely where the mother's own family of origin resided in an urban area. Usually, the father is the bread-winner, either through institutional employment and/or through private holdings.

It has been remarked by several scholars that the early upbringing of the Indo-Pakistani child is more permissive compared to that of his western counterpart (Mandelbaum 1970; Strodtbeck 1971). This agrees well with the culture's concept of the role of the child as a helpless, socially unformed being who cannot be held responsible for his own actions. To be sure, up to a certain point in the life of the child, such a concept of his role must be universally shared among humans. The reason for emphasizing this particular characteristic in the present context is to draw attention to the comparatively much longer period of time that a person is assigned such a role. It would not be difficult to substantiate the assertion that the role of an individual needing guidance and care continues well into adolescence and even adulthood vis-à-vis certain members of one's family. With the child's physical maturity, the emphasis moves onto the personal and social aspects of his self, so that a person's friendships, his marriage, his profession, his mode of interaction with certain sections of the society are not his personal affairs; they are subject to guidance and control from his adults – especially his parents. I should add that this is one of the few aspects of socialization in family which seems to be undergoing a change at the present moment; yet even where total discretion may be allowed, in practice, to an individual, this is often accompanied by a feeling of bitterness and personal failure on the part of his adults – particularly his parents.

In the early stages of a child's life – up to three or four years – the main interaction for purposes of control is most frequently with the mother (like the Western families) and with other close female relatives (unlike the Western families). The patterns of control are normally implicit (Bernstein 1971b); indeed, that mother is regarded as "good" and "fortunate" in the culture, who can control her children by a look in her eyes or by an expression on her face. It follows that elaborate explanations in terms of cause and effect are less frequent, while both threats and emotional bribes are quite common. Rationales are offered in terms of codes of conduct appropriate to a particular sex, a particular age group or by reference to a specific age-relation. The form of interaction amongst the adults of the house provides the child with a model of inter-personal relationships. Although in the last 50 years or so, especially in the urban areas, more families could be said to consist physically of just the parents and their children, it is an oversimplification to think of such a unit as parallel to the Western nuclear family (Mandelbaum 1970). Whatever its physical size and shape, the family in the Indo-Pakistani subcontinent stays moored to this day in the joint family system; the ties between the parents and children and between siblings are close indeed, leading to very frequent interactions in varied contexts, even though not all close relatives may live under the same roof or eat from the same kitchen. Thus the child has enough occasions to observe in the interaction of the adults how such ascribed boundaries as those of sex, age, and kinship affect the patterns of interaction. A child would no more expect to hear his mother answer back or argue with his grandmother, than he would expect himself to answer back or argue with his own mother. His father is no more likely to raise his voice to his elder brother than the child himself is likely to be allowed to disregard the superiority that accrues to his own elder brother by virtue of age. While the authority of the mother is "diffused", since there are no areas in which the mother may control the child but the mother's mother or the father's mother may not, in this very pattern of the diffusion of authority the "inevitable" nature of hierarchically controlled relationships are made real for the child. These clear cut, unblurred boundaries set up by reference to the ascribed attributes of sex, age, and kinship relation "create a strong sense of membership and so a specific identity". For arriving at his identity as a cultural and social being, these close ties in the family are most important, although to date the relationship with the super-natural and the "guru" may be just as important as suggested by Hsu (1963). But, when we explore the bases of these two last relations we find that the dominant principle in the guru relationship conforms to that of hierarchical boundary maintenance, while the relationship to the supernatural is a function of the everyday community-based common sense knowledge. There is no exaggeration in the suggestion that in establishing this relationship, the educational system does not play any important initial part. If we accept Hsu's mode of examining the individual as a cultural and social being, then in the psychosocial homeostasis of the Indo-

Pakistani child, it is the immediate group – the family – that plays the crucial role of determining what affects will belong to his most intimate layer, the one that determines his "human constant" (1971b). The strong framing in the Indo-Pakistani educational system between common sense community-based knowledge and uncommon sense school knowledge, thus, leaves the Indian child untouched. Unlike the West, here, it is not the educational system which plays a crucial role in determining his "human substance"; the fundamental base of his identity as a social and cultural being is complete, independently of the school and the wider peer group. By conforming to the dominant principles of familial socialization, the educational system rather reinforces this sense of identity, seldom creating any new effects which can compete successfully with the effects already created by socialization in the family.

I shall dwell only briefly on another context of socialization in the family: the instructional context (Bernstein 1971c), including within it also "play". Despite the educational status of his parents, typically the child's instruction is a matter for the school and the teacher. Indo-Pakistani parents seldom interfere with the workings of the school; in the majority of cases, especially past the kindergarten stage – which is, in any event, available to a very limited section of the population – the only contact that the parents have with the educational institutions is economic – the paying of fees, fines, and dues and the receiving of progress reports, including examination results, which, up to the secondary stage, are addressed, typically, direct to the parents. If a student is found weak in some subject, a recommendation may be made by the school for extra tuition; and typically this means that a private instructor is hired to coach the student for a set number of hours at his own home. Even this spatial proximity of the teacher – the special instructor – with the parents does not necessarily lead to any but the most perfunctory interaction. The teacher may be entertained as a guest either at the end or beginning of the lesson, but normally one does not discuss the child's specific educational problems or the mode of coping with them. In conformity with this pattern of maintaining a clear boundary between the child's educational school knowledge and the home life, it would be found that the instructional context in the home revolves around skills that are not relevant to what goes on in the school. Studies of American Indian cultures have indicated that, here, instruction inside the family in skills is predominantly implicit: the characteristic mode of learning is "visual" and "physical" (John 1972; Dumont 1972; Phillip 1972). The same could be said about the Indo-Pakistani culture. It is, then, not surprising that play is unstructured and usually not subject to guidance; nor is it surprising that there is a clear cut boundary between play and instruction. Play is not seen as representing a potential for increasing that type of knowledge which is the sole monopoly of the educational institutions. Nonetheless, it would be wrong to suppose that play is not exploited for teaching other orders of relevance, and what is interesting here is the fact that it is used as a vehicle for reinforcing the boundaries which are emphasized in the context of control. Thus after a certain age, a certain type of play is frowned upon; a certain type of play is undesirable, depending upon the sex of the player; at a certain stage mingling of sexes is discouraged in play; and, except in the practical context of helping the mother, the playing of older children of a particular age with the younger ones is seen as a mark of almost total failure in upbringing. The role boundaries are no less clearly delineated here by reference to the ascribed attributes of sex, age, and hierarchy than they are in the context of control.

However we may be inclined to evaluate the patterns of socialization through the family and the educational institutions, sketched partially above, the fact remains that, at a deep level, the two are in essential correspondence with each other and give little or no rise to tension. It is significant that the rate of truancy and other forms of delinquency are comparatively lower here than in the West – and perhaps were lower still a couple of decades ago. I doubt if this could be attributed to the Indo-Pakistani child's great love for learning; to me it seems that the main reason for this lies in the essential symbolic continuity of the two systems of socialization. The strong classification and the strong framing of educational knowledge does not make unreasonable demands from the Indo-Pakistani child in orientation to objects and persons. The symbolic meanings of one do not threaten or question the symbolic meanings of the other; rather they reinforce each other, feeding into the very phenomena which are deeply meaningful to a person, and which, if I interpret Hsu correctly (1971b), belong to his most intimate layer, providing him with a sense of his own identity. Through these correspondences, the Indo-Pakistani educational system is rendered largely safe, so far as cultural change is concerned.

With this rather sketchy account of the relationship between the familial socialization and the educational system, I would like to turn now to the specific problems of the Indo-Pakistani student at, for example, an English university. In the latter too the classification of educational knowledge is strong (Bernstein 1971: 208), though by comparison, it appears to be weaker than the Indo-Pakistani one. The greater difference is to be noticed in the area of framing; especially at the university level, the framing of educational knowledge is much weaker in England than in the subcontinent. The amount of discretion allowed to the student here is much greater; and, to the extent that the classification of knowledge is weaker compared with the subcontinental one, there is a greater degree of emphasis in English universities on "ways of knowing" rather than on "the state of knowledge". The weight of the entire pattern of sociali-zation on the Indo-Pakistani subcontinent runs counter to the increased discretion for the student and to emphasis on ways of knowing. The security of a specific identity which is so carefully, though unconsciously, built into the familial and educational socialization on the subcontinent is challenged by the symbolic significance of the reduced insulation between contents and a blurring of boundaries between the teacher and the taught. In personal discussions with colleagues in England, two comments on the situation come up frequently: teachers sense that a great deal of "mothering" is required to help the student succeed and they are surprised by the unevenness of the Indo-Pakistani student's performance, who can produce a meticulous, first-rate summary of articles and publications, but who flounders when faced with the task of examining critically the assumptions underlying the statements in these very works. I suggest that the former is a mental excercise in which the student is at home, it being the most characteristic form of learning in educational systems with exceptionally strong classification and framing of educational knowledge; the latter form of excercise is as foreign to him as fish and mashed potatoes.

Talking to the so-called serious students, one gets the impression that the Indo-Pakistani student devotes much more time to his studies than his English counterpart; despite this, he is barely able to "keep up" with him. The effects of the greater discretion allowed to the student are overtly expressed by him – especially in the social sciences – as an un-certainty as to what actually is required of him in the way of doing, and what is or is not to be read. Often the students will claim that the subject (content) is just too wide and there is just too much to be learnt: In both cases, it is significant to note that the approach to the problems is me-chanical and quantitative. As the focus is mainly on reading and taking down notes – i.e., preparing summaries of the read material – it is not surprising that we often hear of mechanical difficulties involved in quick reading. Now, it may be true that within this context the Indo-Pakistani student reads English more slowly than the English one, but it is to be questioned whether there is a crucial difference between him and his English peer in the amount of time it takes both to read, say, a thriller. And if there is no crucial difference here, it would follow that it is not the mechanical act of reading English, *per se*, which is responsible for the slow reading in the domain of the selected content. At this point, it may appear that the Indo-Pakistani student is perhaps less able to "receive" the contents than the English student. One's judgement on this score would depend upon how one approaches the question of the content. A good Indo-Pakistani student can, and often does, compete successfully with his good English peer in summarizing the contents of an article. The difference is most noticeable in two areas: (i) when it comes to stating why a certain hypothesis is put forward and how it is arrived at, the English student would normally do better, and equally (ii) when the student is expected to explore the implications of some specific hypothesis – what extrapolation can be made from it – he is again likely to do less well than the English student. This would seem to be suggestive of a difference in the orientation to the entire question of what is considered "content" – the "object of knowledge"; and, perhaps, this ought not to be confused with just assimilating the gist of the content. The real problem is not so much the problem of how to read and how to "understand" – i.e., literally decode the messages. The real problem would rather appear to be in knowing how and why one should proceed in which direction, given that the message has been understood as "saying" such and such. The difficulties arise from not being able to find out – or orient oneself to – ways of knowing, rather than from collecting elements of that which is to be known.

It would seem, then, that, at a very deep level, cross-cultural education of the type under discussion becomes a process of redefinition of his identity for the Indo-Pakistani student. The English educational system at the university level questions these very dominant principles which went into defining his perception of self as a cultural and social being. It is significant that in the last half century there has been a growth in fiction, centering around the theme of alienation, where the alienated person is no other than our successful Indo-Pakistani scholar who has returned from abroad after years of sojourn in England. It is tempting to ask whether there is a subconscious realization here that to be a successful scholar in Britain an Indo-Pakistani person must radically change as a person. It is again interesting to note that the problems which arise for the alienated character in these works of fiction are just those which relate to the "self-defining boundaries" such as those of hierarchy, sex, age, and religion, in the native culture.

SUMMARY

(1) Following Bernstein, I have argued that educational systems are intricately related to the culture in which they are embedded;
(2) I have attempted to show that socialization through the family and the educational institutions on the subcontinent creates a particular sense of "identity";
(3) I have argued that this identity is challenged when the student is brought into the English educational system at the university level and that it is this conflict that gives rise to many intangible problems in cross-cultural education;
(4) I have argued that whereas the mechanical problems arising from the educational process are better understood, and perhaps better solved, there is so far no evidence that problems that arise from the deep symbolic differences between two distinct educational systems have been made explicit.

In my discussion I have leaned heavily on hypotheses put forward by Bernstein and by Hsu. I claim total responsibility for the interpretation and application of their hypotheses.

Northwestern University

REFERENCES

Bernstein, Basil (1971a), "Classification and framing of educational knowledge", in: *Class, Codes and Control*, Vol. 1, ed. by B. Bernstein. London, Routledge & Kegan Paul.
— (1971b), "A sociolinguistic approach to socialization: with some reference to educability", in: *Class, Codes and Control*, Vol. 1, ed. by B. Bernstein. London, Routledge & Kegan Paul.
— (1971c), "A critique of the concept of compensatory education", in: *Class, Codes and Control*, Vol. 1, ed. by B. Bernstein. London, Routledge & Kegan Paul.
Brown, R., and Lenneberg, E. H. (1954), "A study in language and cognition", *Journal of Abnormal and Social Psychology* 49 (3).
Douglas, Mary (1972), "Self-evidence" (Henry Myers Lecture 1972), *Proceedings of the R.A.I.*
Dumont, Robert V. (1972), "Learning English and how to be silent: studies in Sioux and Cherokee classroom", in: *Functions of Language in the Classroom*, ed. by C. B. Cazden, V. P. John, and D. Hymes. New York, Columbia University Press.
Firth, J. R. (1957), "A synopsis of linguistic theory 1935–55", in: *Studies in Linguistic Analysis*. Oxford, Blackwell.
Fishman, J. A. (1972), *The Sociology of Language* (section viii). Rowley, Mass., Newbury House Publishers, Inc.

Hoijer, H. (1948), "Linguistic and cultural change", *Language* 24.

Hsu, Francis L. K. (1963), *Clan, Caste and Club*. Princeton, N. J., D. Van Norstrand Co., Inc.

— (ed.) (1971a), *Kinship and Culture*. Chicago, Aldine Publishing Co.

— (1971b), "Psychosocial homeostasis and jen: conceptual tools for advancing psychological anthropology", *American Anthropologist* 73 (1).

John, Vera P. (1972), "Style of learning – style of teaching: reflections on the education of Navajo children", in: *Functions of Language in the Classroom*, ed. by C. B. Cazden, V. P. John and D. Hymes. New York, Columbia University Press.

Kluckhohn, Clyde, and Kelly, W. (1945), "The concept of culture", in: *The Science of Man in the World Crisis*, ed. by R. Linton. New York, Columbia University Press.

Mandelbaum, David G. (1970), *Society in India*, Vols. 1 and 2. Berkeley, University of California Press.

Phillips, Susan U. (1972), "Participant structures and communicative competence: Warm Springs children in the community classroom", in: *Foundations of Language in the Classroom*, ed. by C. B. Cazden, V. P. John, and D. Hymes. New York, Columbia University Press.

Strodtbeck, Fred L. (1971), "Sex-role, identity and dominant kinship relations", in: *Kinship and Culture*, ed. by Francis L. K. Hsu. Chicago, Aldine Publishing Co.

Whorf, Benjamin L. (1956), *Language, Thought and Reality*, ed. by John B. Carroll. Cambridge, Mass., M.I.T. Press.

LAWRENCE D. CARRINGTON

Determining Language Education Policy
In Caribbean Sociolinguistic Complexes*

Numerous researchers have reported on the interaction between languages in Caribbean territories. Few have attempted statements of appropriate determinations of language education policy for the same region. This paper attempts to focus on factors which might inform such policies in territories where a creole language interacts with other languages having recognised standards.

   The region under scrutiny includes those territories in which creole languages are the media of internal communication among the major part of the population, starting in the north-west in Belize on the Central American mainland, stretching through the Antillean archipelago to the Guianas and including Aruba, Bonaire, and Curaçao. This excludes Cuba, Santo Domingo, and Puerto Rico where the varieties of Spanish spoken have not been identified as creolized. The region is characterized by mismatch between the official languages and the languages of wider communication. English, French, and Dutch are official languages but the populations speak creoles with English, French, and Spanish-Portuguese lexical bases, Hindi-Urdu, Spanish, and to a lesser extent Chinese, Javanese, and Amerindian languages.

DISTRIBUTION OF LANGUAGES

Accurate statement of the geographical distribution and extent of use of languages in the region is made hazardous by the following:

(a)   Only in the cases of Papiamentu, Sranan, and Saramakkan do the Creoles have distinctive official labels which do not name the

* The author acknowledges the comments of his colleagues Clive Borely and Robin Kesterton during the preparation of the paper.

lexical source of the language. Hence, in all except Dutch territory, the labels applied to the languages may obscure the difference between the standard and a creole.

(b) The term "English", when used to refer to the language of former British territories where English-lexicon Creoles occur, includes the foreign standard, educated local standard, and the creole.

(c) The ability to speak the European official language is prestigious. As a result when asked about his language use, an individual may state that he speaks the official language even though an objective assessment may show him to be marginally competent in that language.

(d) The last census that noted language information for the then British territories (and even then not for all) was in 1946. Furthermore, linguistic awareness was not fully awake at the official level when the censuses were taken, and is even now still dormant at the popular level. Since many people who speak creole genuinely believe they speak the European standard, figures would probably have been misleading.

English and English-Lexicon Creoles

In Jamaica, English is the official language but the medium of wider communication is Jamaican Creole and a set of interdialects in a speech continuum between the basilect[1] and Standard English. In the British Associated States of Antigua, St. Kitts-Nevis-Anguilla, Montserrat and St. Vincent, and in the independent state of Barbados, English is the official language. The languages of the populations are as many varieties of a Creole whose lexicon is predominantly English and which freely admits new English items into its repertoire. The languages of these islands have not been described in any way as closely as that of Haiti or of Jamaica. In the newly independent state of Grenada, English is the official language but the vernacular language is an English-lexicon Creole showing evidence of formerly widespread use of French-lexicon Creole which has all but disappeared.

English and French Creole

St. Lucia and Dominica, both formerly British colonies and now Associated States, are obvious cases of mismatch between official language and popular language. Here too, English is official but the majority of the population uses a French-lexicon Creole[2] akin to that of Haiti as the language of daily communication. The 1946 census listed 24.9% of Dominicans and 43.4% of St. Lucians as speakers of Creole exclusively. In addition, 68.3% of Dominicans and 54% of St. Lucians were listed as bilingual. In 1966, I estimated that the number of bilinguals had increased in both cases with a consequent drop in the number of monolingual Creole speakers.

French and French Creole

Haiti, the Caribbean's first republic, continues to recognize French as its official language but the language most widely used is French-lexicon Creole[3]. Estimates of the extent of use of Creole vary between 80% and 90% of the population. In the French departments of Martinique and Guadeloupe, French is official and French-lexicon Creole[4] is the popular language. No figures are available for numbers of Creole speakers. French Guiana repeats the pattern of Martinique and Guadeloupe.

More complex cases

In Belize, English is the official language. Allsopp (1965) indicates that in 1960, of the population over 15 years old, 50.8% were speakers of English (i.e., educated standard and Creole) 30.8% speakers of Spanish, 10.2% of Mayan, and 8.2% of Carib. As in Belize, in Trinidad and Tobago, English is the official language. French Creole[5] persists in northern mountain areas as well as in fishing villages along the east and south coasts. Spanish[6] co-exists with French Creole as the first language of a small number of elderly persons. Far more important is Hindi-Urdu[7] for which no census figures are available. However, a reasonable estimate can be made on the basis of the fact that 40% of the population is of Indian ancestry. Carrington, Borely, and Knight (1974) report on a recent survey of the languages to which primary school-children between the ages of 5 and 11 years are exposed in the familial environment in Trinidad.[8] The study shows that 46.4% of the sample were exposed to Hindi-Urdu either as speakers of the language, by being addressed in it or by hearing it spoken in the household. The lingua franca of Trinidad is an English-lexicon Creole[9] showing evidence of former use of French

Creole. The lingua franca of Tobago[10] shows marked similarity to Jamaican Creole. In Guyana the official language, English, yields place of daily usage to Guyanese English-lexicon Creole.[11] Hindi-Urdu is also widely used among persons of Indian ancestry who constitute nearly

TABLE I

Showing Distribution of Languages in Region

Country	Official language	Popular language	Other major	Other minor
Jamaica	Eng.	Jamaican Creole Eng-lex.	–	–
Antigua St. Kitts- Nevis- Anguilla Montserrat St. Vincent Barbados Grenada	Eng.	Eng-lex. Creoles	–	–
St. Lucia	Eng.	Fr.-Lex.	–	–
Dominica	Eng.	Creole	–	–
Haiti	Fr.	Fr.-lex.	–	–
Martinique	Fr.	Creole	–	–
Guadeloupe	Fr.	Creole	–	–
French Guiana	Fr.	Creole	–	–
Belize	Eng.	Eng.-lex. Creole	Spanish	Mayan
Trinidad & Tobago	Eng.	Eng.-lex. Creole	Hindi- Urdu	Fr.-lex. Creole
Guyana	Eng.	Creole	Urdu	–
Surinam	Dutch	Sranan	Hindi- Urdu Javanese	Saram- akkan Chinese
Aruba, Bonaire Cuaçao	Dutch	Papia- mentu Sp.-Port.- lex.	–	–

one-half of the population.[12] The third complex case is that of Surinam. Dutch, the official language, is spoken natively by a mere 1.5% of the population. Sranan Tongo, [13] an English-lexicon Creole is spoken by 38% of the population, Saramakkan, also an English-lexicon Creole, by 9%, Hindi-Urdu by 35%, Javanese languages by 13%, and Chinese by 1.5%. Aruba, Bonaire, and Curaçao share with Surinam the official Dutch language, but Papiamentu,[14] a Spanish-Portuguese-lexicon Creole, functions as the language of wider communication.

In summary then (see Table I), where English is the official language, except for St. Lucia and Dominica, English-lexicon Creoles are the lingua franca. Where French is the official language, French-lexicon Creole is the language of the masses. In St. Lucia and Dominica, this language also functions as the language of the people. Where Dutch is official, two distinct English-lexicon Creoles and a Spanish-Portuguese Creole are the languages of wider communication. Hindi-Urdu is used by large minorities in Trinidad, Surinam, and Guyana. Spanish is the lingua franca of northern Belize. Javanese languages are used by a minority in Surinam.

FUNCTIONAL RELATIONSHIP AND STATUS OF THE LANGUAGES

Throughout the region the use of the official language is prestigious, but this does not imply that the official language is always viewed as appropriate. The other languages in use begin by being private-informal situation languages and the extent to which they are used outside of this area varies from one territory/language to another.

The world status languages

For purposes of this discussion it is useful to differentiate between the languages of world status, i.e., Spanish and Hindi-Urdu, and the Creoles. None of the situations in which these languages interact with the official languages and languages of wider communication has been sufficiently described to allow unchallengeable statements. Indeed Ashcroft and Jones (1966) point out that Allsopp (1965) oversimplified the relationship in Belize. However, in view of the political orientation, whether superficial or not, of Belize to Guatemala, Spanish, although a minority group language, would enjoy sufficient prestige that its use in formal situations would not meet with disapproval in the area where it is the lingua franca.

The position of Hindi-Urdu is somewhat different. In those territories where it is spoken, it is specifically bound to one ethnic group, (no one outside the group normally learns to speak it) and linked to cultural traditions which are not shared by any other group. It functions within the ethno-cultural group to the extent that the group retains its cultural traditions in the face of societal pressures which erode non-Western life styles. It seems clear that in Trinidad at least, and more than likely in Guyana and Surinam, Hindi-Urdu is not widely used by the younger generation of Indians. The relationship between it and the languages of wider communication with which it is in contact therefore falls within the scope of normal bilingualism.

The Creole languages

The interaction of the creole languages with the official languages has been more adequately described. The prototype description is embodied in Ferguson (1959) in which he uses the relationship between Haitian Creole and French as an example of diglossia. With a fair degree of consistency the model holds for those societies which have been studied. Stewart (1962 and 1963) suggests two axes on which the relationship might be plotted – I Public-Private, II Formal-Informal. He shows the official language functioning in the public-formal sector with the Creole in the private-informal sector leaving an area of fluctuation between the two in the private-formal and public-informal situations. Discussions by Carrington (1967) on St. Lucia, and Eersel (1971) on Surinam indicate that relative social status of speakers affects language choice.

Written literature in the creole languages is limited and with the exception of Papiamentu, orthographic systems are not widely known among speakers of the creoles. Stewart (1962) summarises and firmly rejects the commonly held attitudes towards creoles, but it is worthwhile to note them here:

(a)   Creole is not a language;
(b)   Creole has no grammar; it is a made-up form of speech;
(c)   Creole is a corruption of the lexically related standard;
(d)   Creole has no uniformity of usage;
(e)   Creole is a mixture of many languages.

Of more importance, too, in the interaction of Creoles with official languages is the phenomenon of code switching. Indeed this is a primary characteristic of the use of the languages.

Change in attitudes

The movement towards independence of the territories in the region has been accompanied by rejection of external symbols of former colonial status. Together with the hemisphere-wide consciousness shift towards "people power", regionally expressed as "black power", this has affected the orderliness with which attitudes towards the official languages and the Creoles can be stated. Indeed, it is now prestigious and fashionable to use Creole for purposes which might otherwise have called for the official language. At the moment, though, this a conscious level protest decision which does not necessarily change the underlying attitudes.

CHANGE IN LANGUAGE EDUCATION POLICY

Current policy

The degree to which Creoles have been recognised for educational purposes has varied over the years and from one territory to the next. By and large, in terms of Kloss' (1968) juridical typology they have been either "proscribed" or "tolerated". Formal proscription is reported by Lastra (1968) in the French areas.

In the French areas, the use of the vernacular is forbidden in the classroom. . . .

Even where formal proscription was not a fact, aggressive attitudes of rejection have for years been common among teachers. Alleyne (1961) records the case of a teacher in St. Lucia who in the 1920's made the rounds of an east-coast village whipping any child whom he heard speaking Creole. At a higher and presumably less personalized level, the attitude of a Barbadian education officer in St. Lucia is reported by Verin (1958).

"Certain general directions were sent to St. Lucia by UNESCO and among them it was stated explicitly that no educational policy should tend to eradicate local language. The Education Officer, a Barbadian, sententiously declared, 'But these instructions do not in any way concern us since Creole is not a language' ".

These examples can be repeated for several other territories as any one who has grown up in the West Indies would know. But the overtness with which anti-Creole attitudes have expressed themselves has been tempered within recent times. Lastra (1968), at the same time that she records the proscription of Creole in schools of the French territories, notes that provision is made in Surinam for bilingual schools.[15] No such provision is made in territories where English is the official language. Nevertheless, the official position has not been static. Compare the following extracts from school syllabuses in Trinidad and Tobago. The foreword to the language Syllabus for Primary Schools 1946[16] states in part:

In this country where the impact of various foreign languages has greatly influenced the common forms of speech and expression and has considerably increased the teacher's task, every opportunity must be taken both in school and out of school and in the formal English or other lessons to correct common errors of speech as they occur; otherwise faulty expression or construction may in the child's mind acquire the sanction of usage.

By comparison, the current syllabus for English in the Junior Secondary Schools states:

The Junior Secondary Syllabus for English recognises that there is a double language situation in Trinidad where the first language is a dialect of English spoken by the vast majority of its children and the official language of the country is standard English. It recognises the problems of interference that operate when the Trinidadian pupils attempt to learn English and it attempts by the methodology suggested and the emphasis laid down to facilitate the learning process as much as possible.

In similar vein, the English syllabus for Grades 7–9 in Jamaica states:

English is the official language of Jamaica. Nearly all our children first learn to speak Jamaican Creole, which has taken nearly all its vocabulary from English but much of its syntax from other sources; but in order to play a productive role in modern Jamaican society, they must be able to communicate effectively and accurately in English. We must strive to make Jamaican children highly competent in the language most widely spoken in the world, while teaching them to appreciate the local Creole (p. 1).

The Jamaican syllabus goes even further to accommodate Creole:

In view of the fluid language situation in Jamaica, teachers are expected to adopt a common-sense and humane attitude to what is acceptable in the local society; it is pedantic to insist on a particular British-English structure when it is clear that such a structure is rarely or never employed by educated Jamaicans (p. 2).

Limitations of current practice

The orientation of the syllabus referred to is somewhat ahead of the training levels and linguistic sophistication of the teachers who are to implement them and most importantly ahead of the attitudes which they hold privately on the question of language acceptability. But the effect of the official directives is to increase the frequency of the question – what should be the language of instruction? The mass of the teaching force in Jamaica and Trinidad would react to the syllabus preambles favourably, not because it reflects their views but because they would feel old-fashioned if they did not accept it. The problems arise in the interpretation of terms such as "local Creole", "acceptable in the local society" and "educated Jamaicans". Certainly, in the Eastern Caribbean islands where English is the official language, my recent experience with teachers has been that there is a feeling of anxiety, insecurity and helplessness over how to put into practice the enlightened views presented to them by language education specialists.

DETERMINING LANGUAGE EDUCATION POLICY

It is against the background described that the question is posed: what should be the languages of instruction in the schools of the region? This paper proposes that policy decisions should be based on the following considerations:

(a) linguistic relationship of the popular languages to the official language;
(b) the degree to which a continuum is present;
(c) identifiability of a norm acceptable to the population;
(d) level of nation consciousness;
(e) geographical and age distribution of languages.

Statement of principles

For purposes of the discussion the region may be divided into cases in which the languages of the people are unrelated to the official languages and cases where they are related. (See Table II).

TABLE II

Showing Relationship of Languages of Wide Communication to Official Languages

	Eng.-lex. Creole as LWC	Fr.-lex. Creoles as LWC	Sp.-Port. Creole as LWC	Hindi-Urdu	Spanish	Indigenous Amerindian
Related to official language	Belize, Jamaica, Antigua, St. Kitts-Nevis Anguilla, Montserrat Barbados, St. Vincent, Grenada, Trinidad & Tobago, Guyana	Haiti, Fr. Guiana, Martinique, Guadeloupe				
Not related to official language	Surinam	St. Lucia, Dominica	Aruba, Bonaire, Curaçao	Guyana, Trinidad & Tobago, Surinam	Belize	Belize

Principle I.   Where a language is *unrelated* to the official language, conditions are linguistically *favourable* for its use as a medium of instruction. Where a language is *related* to the official language, conditions are linguistically *unfavourable* for its use as a medium of instruction.

Application of this principle in Table II would have the effect of admitting the following languages to use as media of instruction in the territories stated: Sranan in Surinam, Creole French in St. Lucia and Dominica, Papiamentu in Aruba, Bonaire, and Curaçao, Hindi-Urdu in Trinidad and Tobago, Surinam and Guyana, Spanish in Belize, indigenous Amerindian languages in Belize. It would also exclude the use of English-lexicon Creoles in all of the region except Surinam and of French-lexicon Creoles in Haiti and the French territories.

Principle II.   Where a *post-Creole continuum* links the official language
to a lexically related Creole, conditions are *unfavourable*
for the use of that Creole as a medium of instruction.
Where there is *no post-Creole continuum*, conditions are
favourable for the use of that Creole as a medium of
instruction.

Table III shows the distribution of continua.

TABLE III

Continuum identified and partially described	No Continuum described	
	Continuum suspected	No continuum suspected
Jamaica	All other Eng. official areas (except	Rural
Guyana	St. Lucia and Dominica), Martinique,	Haiti
	Guadeloupe, Fr. Guiana, Urban Haiti	

This principle has an intrinsic snag: that the identification and description of a continuum is the result of a theoretical approach to the study of variation. Consequently, it depends upon which linguist describes the communication complex in the given territory. For example, a complex described by Bickerton will more than likely show a continuum whereas one described by Solomon[17] will more than likely show no continuum. Table III also introduces the notion of internal geographical distribution of the varieties of a given Creole. Indeed the question of distribution applies as well to languages which are unrelated to the official language (see Principle V).

The unfavourable nature of the continuum situation resides in several factors. Firstly, there is the difficulty of drawing the dividing line between the official language and upper-end continuum varieties. For the layman, the problem is related to the view of creoles as badly spoken or corrupted forms of the lexically related standard language. Interdialects of the continuum are therefore seen as "better" or "worse" forms of the related standard. Furthermore, in the continuum type situation, even among teachers, the population's notion of the Standard language is hazy.[18]

For the linguist, even one who is prepared to recognise a continuum, the proplem is to define levels within the continuum at each of which *'tout se tient'*; that is, in terms of co-occurrence restrictions, a level identified must be characteristic of a community/group within the society. The social repercussions of selection of a norm for the Creole cannot be ignored. The determination of a given level of the continuum as a norm for the Creole by extra-linguistic factors implies the selection of a social group whose speech would be analysed. There can be vociferous reaction to the choice of any group on the grounds of it being too low or too high. This leads to considerations under Principle III.

Principle III.   Where (i)   a norm for a Creole is identified,
                 and   (ii)   this norm is acceptable to the population,
                 and   (iii)   this norm is *in layman's terms*, perceptibly
                                distinct from the lexically related standard,
                 conditions are favourable for use of that norm as the
                 medium of instruction, *provided that* the size of the
                 population using that variety as their normal means of
                 communication is compatible with the number of
                 persons to be instructed through the medium.

This proviso is important because although a population may on a nation-wide basis, accept a stated norm as *the* norm for a Creole, significant sections of that population may not consider themselves speakers of this norm; they may reject the idea of education through this medium as retrogressive. This sentiment is founded on the anti-Creole prejudices that feed on the slave-society genesis of these languages in the region.

Principle IV.   Where the societal value-system of a given country are
                inner-directed, conditions are *favourable* for the use of a
                Creole as the medium of instruction. Where the societal
                value systems are *outer-directed*, conditions are *not
                favourable* for the use of a Creole as the medium of
                instruction.

This may appear to be an odd principle. It may be argued that the common regional interest in catching up with the rest of the world may indicate outer-directed value systems. But recent developments in societal change in the region suggest that some of the territories, (e.g., Jamaica and Guyana) have gained or are gaining sufficient confidence as nation-states with an identity to be moving towards inner-directed value systems. Others may be operating with inner-directed value systems by virtue of not having moved into the mainstream of modernity (e.g., Haiti). On the other hand the French domination of Martinique may be sufficient to make that island outer-directed despite localised ideological rejection of metropolitan control.

Principle V.   Where the speakers of a given language are *geographically concentrated*, conditions are *favourable* for the use of that language as a medium of instruction. Where they are *geographically dispersed*, conditions are *unfavourable* for the use of that language as a medium of instruction.

The principle is simple and requires little elaboration. Its application to Table II would, for example, make Spanish a strong contender in northern Belize. The point is that geographical concentration would offer the group sufficient internal viability to facilitate acceptance of a language of instruction other than the official language. Similarly on a geographical basis, French Creole might be recommended as a medium of instruction in Haiti.

Principle VI.   Where a language other than the official language continues to be spoken as a first language by the population at whom the education programme is aimed, conditions are favourable for its use as a medium of instruction (but see Principle I).

According to this principle, in the case of Hindi-Urdu in Trinidad and in Guyana, conditions may not be favourable since there may be insufficient numbers of the school-age population who *speak* the language to necessitate its use as a medium of instruction. For purposes of adult education however the question is much more open.

These principles may be used to test the linguistic and sociological soundness of a decision to use a language other than the official language as a medium of instruction. The feasibility of implementing such a decision will clearly have to relate to other considerations. Included in these would be the cost of

(i)   provision of instructional materials;
(ii)   the training of the teachers;
(iii)   the public education programme that should precede implementation.

A corollary of the decision to use a given language as a medium of instruction is that the official language would then be taught as a second language. This would also have cost implications for the training of the teaching force. It should be noted though that the use of a hitherto unofficial language need not be throughout the whole system of education. The language chosen should be used in as many grades of the school system as are necessary for pupils to acquire a working knowledge of the official language *appropriate to their age and stage of maturity.* Hence it is not reasonable to say from the outset that only primary education or only the first two years of education should be in the new medium of instruction. Each case will have to set its targets and revise them in the light of results.

CONCLUSION

The paper proposes six principles that may be applied within the Caribbean region to determine whether a language other than the official language of a territory should be used, as a matter of educational policy, as a medium of instruction. The principles stand on the basis of the linguistic relationships and sociolinguistic interaction of the languages as well as on the social attitudes towards them.[19] No relative weighting of the principles is suggested although this is in fact of crucial importance. The statistical weighting of intangibles of socio-cultural interaction is an extraordinarily difficult and specialist task which falls outside the author's competence. It is hoped that some other researcher may be able to suggest a weighting method.

University of the West Indies
St. Augustine, Trinidad.

NOTES

1. For description of Jamaican Creole and comments on the continuum, see Le Page and De Camp (1960), Cassidy (1961), Bailey (1966), Cassidy and Le Page (1967), De Camp (1968), Craig (1968).
2. For description of St. Lucian, see Carrington (1967), and Valdman and Carrington (1969). For Dominican, see Taylor (1947, 1951), and Christie (1969).
3. For description of Haitian, see Comhaire-Sylvain (1936), Hall (1953), D'Ans (1968).
4. For description of Martiniquan, see Funk (1950, 1953), Jourdain (1956), Carter (1960). For description of Guadeloupean, see Nainsouta (1940).

5. For description of Trinidadian French Creole, see Thomas (1869 and 1969).
6. For description and comments on Trinidad Spanish see, Thompson (1957) and Moodie (1970).
7. The major variety of Hindi-Urdu spoken is Bhojpuri. There are small numbers of speakers of the Dravidian languages, Tamil and Telegu.
8. The paper referred to did not have as its major purpose a survey of language use. The questionnaire used was a crude instrument for determining exposure since no information about frequency of usage or degree of competence was sought. Furthermore, sampling was based on the distribution of schools throughout the island rather than on distribution of population in the age group under study.
9. For descriptions, see Solomon (1966), Warner (1967), Winford (1972).
10. For similarities to Jamaican, see James (1974).
11. For descriptions and comments on the continuum, see Allsopp (1958, 1962) Bickerton (1970, 1971, 1972).
12. Rustow (1968) lists at Table 2 (p. 101), 45% of the Guyana population as speakers of Hindi-Urdu. The figure is plausible but is open to question in view of the inaccuracy of his source on three other counts, viz. in Table 1 (p. 96), 1% Spanish for Barbados, 1% Spanish for Jamaica, and 2% Hindi-Urdu for Trinidad. His source was S. I. Bruk, ed., *Chislennost'i Rasselenie Naradov Mira* (Moscow, Izdatel'stvo Akademii Nauk S.S.R., Institut Etnografii, 1962).
13. For description, see notably Hall (1948), Rens (1953), Voorhoeve (1957, 1962).
14. For description see, among others, Goilo (1953).
15. A linguist who knows Surinam in detail has indicated in a private communication that the provision is more impressive on paper than in practice. In view of this, I have not placed Sranan in the category "promoted" of Kloss Typology.
16. Incidentally this syllabus has not yet been replaced although several new drafts have been prepared.
17. See Solomon (1972).
18. Observations by Le Page (1968), p. 437 are relevant here.
19. A linguist who knows the Caribbean scene well once threatened me with the dire fate of being "crucified on the dialect cross" for allowing such social considerations to subvert linguistic truth. However I feel sure that following through the linguistic truths without great sensitivity to the sociological considerations could result in serious social upheaval.

REFERENCES

Alleyne, M. C. (1961), "Language and Society in St. Lucia", *Caribbean Studies* 1 (1):1–10.
Allsopp, S. R. R. (1958), "Pronominal forms in the dialect of English used in Georgetown (British Guyana) and its environs by people engaged in non-clerical occupations". Unpublished M. A. thesis, University of London.
— (1962), "Expression of state and action in the dialect of English used in the Georgetown area of British Guyana". Unpublished Ph. D. dissertation, University of London.
— (1965), "British Honduras – the linguistic dilemma", *Caribbean Quarterly* 2 (3 & 4):54–61.
Ashcroft, N., and Jones, G. (1966), "Linguistic Problems in British Honduras", *Caribbean Quarterly* 12 (4):55–7.
Bailey, B. L. (1966), *Jamaican Creole Syntax: A Transformational Approach*. Cambridge, Cambridge University Press.

Bickerton, D. (1970), "Some Problems of Linguistic Variation in a Dialect Continuum". Paper read at Conference of Caribbean Linguistics, U.W.I., Trinidad, 1970.
— (1971), "Inherent variability and variable rules", *Foundations of Language* 7:457–92.
— (1971a), "On the Nature of a Creole Continuum". Paper read at Conference of Caribbean Linguistics, Jamaica, 1971.
— (1972), "System into System". Presented at Conference on Creole Languages and Educational Development, U.W.I., St. Augustine, July 1972.
Carrington, L. D. (1967), "St. Lucien Creole: a descriptive analysis of its phonolgy and morpho-syntax". Unpublished Ph. D. dissertation, U.W.I.
Carrington, L. D., Borely, C. B., and Knight, H. E. (1974), "Linguistic exposure of Trinidadian children", to appear in: *Caribbean Journal of Education.*
Carter, M. E. (1960), "Segmental phonemes of Martinique Creole". Unpublished Masters thesis, Georgetown University.
Cassidy, F. G. (1961), *Jamaica Talk: Three Hundred Years of the English Language in Jamaica.* New York, Macmillan.
Cassidy, F. G., and Le Page, R. B. (1967), *Dictionary of Jamaican English.* Cambridge, Cambridge University Press.
Christie, P. (1969), "A sociolinguistic study of some Dominican Creole speakers". Unpublished Ph. D. dissertation, University of York.
Comhaire-Sylvain, S. (1936), *Le Créole Haitien, morphologie et syntaxe.* Port-au-Prince.
Craig, D. R. (1968), "Education and Creole English in the West Indies and some sociolinguistic factors", pp. 371–91 in: *Pidginization and Creolization of Languages,* ed. by D. Hymes. Cambridge, Cambridge University Press.
D'Ans, A. M. (1968), *Le Créole français d'Haiti.* The Hague, Mouton.
Das Gupta, J. (1968), "Language diversity and national development", pp. 17–26 in: *Language Problems of Developing Nations,* ed. by J. A. Fishman, G. A. Fergusson, and J. Das Gupta. New York, J. Wiley.
De Camp, D. (1968), "Toward a generative analysis of a post-Creole continuum", pp. 349–70 in: Hymes, D.
Eersel, C. (1971), "Prestige in choice of language and linguistic forms", in: Hymes, D.
Ferguson, C. (1959), "Diglossia", *Word* 15 (2):325–40.
Fishman, J. A., Ferguson, C. A., and Das Gupta, J. (1968), *Language Problems of Developing Nations.* New York, J. Wiley.
Funk, H. (1950), "The French Creole dialect of Martinique phonology and morphology". Unpublished Masters essay, University of Virginia.
— (1953), "The French Creole dialect of Martinique". Unpublished Ph.D. dissertation. University of Virginia.
Goilo, E. R. (1953), *Gramatica Papiamentu.* Curaçao, Hollandsche Boeckhandel.
Hall, R. A. (1948), "The linguistic structure of Taki-Taki", *Language* 24:92–116.
— (1953), *Haitian Creole.* Philadelphia, American Folklore Society.
Hymes, D. (ed.) (1971), *Pidginization and Creolization of Languages.* Cambridge, Cambridge University Press.
James, W. (1974), "Some similarites between Jamaican Creole and the dialect of Tobago". Unpublished undergraduate study, U.W.I.
Jourdain, E. (1956), *Du Français aux parlers Créoles.* Paris, Klincksieck.
Kloss, H. (1968), "Notes concerning a language nation typology", in: Fishman, Ferguson, and Das Gupta.
Lastra, Y. (1968), "Literacy", pp. 415–63 in: *Current Trends in Linguistics IV,* ed. by Sebeok. The Hague, Mouton.
Le Page, R. B. (1968), "Problems to be faced in the use of English as the medium of education in the West Indies", pp. 431–42 in: Fishman, Ferguson, and Das Gupta.

Le Page, R. B., and De Camp, D. (1960), *Jamaican Creole: An Historical Introduction to Jamaican Creole.* New York, Macmillan.

Moodie, S. M. (1970), "El Español hablado en Trinidad". Unpublished Ph.D. dissertation, University of Madrid.

Nainsowta, R. (1940), *La Langue Créole.* Basse-Terre.

Rens, L. L. E. (1953), *The Historical and Social Background of Surinam's Negro English.* Amsterdam, North Holland Publishing Co.

Rustow, D. (1968), "Language, modernization and nationhood – an attempt at typology", pp. 87–105 in: Fishman, Ferguson, and Das Gupta.

Solomon, D. V. (1966), "The system of predication in the speech of Trinidad – a quantitative study in decreolization". Unpublished M. A. thesis, Columbia University.

— (1972), "Form, Content and the Post-Creole Continuum". Presented at Conference on Greole Languages and Educational Development, U.W.I., St. Augustine, 1972.

Stewart, W. A. (1962), "Creole languages in the Caribbean", pp. 34–53 in: *Study of the Role of Second Languages in Asia, Africa and Latin America,* by W. A. Rice. Washington, D.C., Center for Applied Linguistics.

— (1963), "The functional distribution of Creole and French in Haiti", pp. 149–62 in: *Linguistics and Language Study,* ed. by G. G. Woodworth. Georgetown University Monograph Series on Language and Linguistics No. 15.

Taylor, D. R. (1947), "Phonemes of Caribbean Creole", *Word* 3:172–79.

— (1951), "Structural outline of Caribbean Creole", *Word* 7:43–61.

Thomas, J. J. (1969), *The Theory and Practice of Creole Grammar.* London, New Beacon Books. (Originally published Port-of-Spain, 1869.)

Thompson, R. W. (1951), "A preliminary survey of the Spanish dialect of Trinidad", *Orbis* Tome III, No. 2:353–71.

Valdman, A., and Carrington, L. (1969), *St. Lucia Creole Basic Course.* Washington, D.C., Peace Corps.

Verin, P. (1958), "The rivalry of Creole and English in the West Indies", *De West Indische Gids* No. 38:163–67.

Voorhoeve, J. (1957), "The verbal system of Sranan", *Lingua* 6 (4):374–96.

— (1962), *Sranan Syntax.* Amsterdam, North Holland Publishing Co.

Warner, M. P. (1967), "Language in Trinidad with special reference to English". Unpublished Masters Philosophy thesis, University of York.

Winford, D. (1972), "A sociolinguistic description of two communities in Trinidad". Unpublished Doctor of Philosophy dissertation, University of York.

DONALD WINFORD

Teacher Attitudes Toward Language Varieties in a Creole Community

It is only recently that students of West Indian Creole languages began turning their attention to the applications that their work might have to the educational problems of Creole communities in the Caribbean. Most of this attention has been focussed on the former British colonies of the area, where varieties of English, ranging from Creole of various forms to standard dialects, make up the communication matrix. It is now commonly accepted that such communities "face social and educational problems directly attributable to the fact that forms of English Creole speech are the everyday language of the majority of their populations" (Craig 1971: 371).

As in the very similar case of Black American English, the full extent of the task before the linguist who tackles such problems in West Indian communities has only just begun to emerge. Baratz (1970) has offered a fairly comprehensive idea of the training and information that must be provided for the teacher of standard English in particular. These include, for instance,

(a) Training in linguistics, with emphasis on such specific areas as interference theory, the influence of social factors on language and language learning, foreign language teaching techniques, etc.
(b) Detailed descriptions of children's vernacular.
(c) Information concerning the social and cultural contexts of language use.
(d) Data on language variation, the factors influencing it and the attitude of people towards it.

It is of course important to identify the areas of variation within a creole continuum,[1] and to define linguistically the differences in linguistic structure involved. But researchers in the field of education have long recognized the importance for language learning of historical and sociological factors such as isolation, discrimination and the different value systems which obtain for various subcultural groups. Linguists have endeavoured for many years to show that differences in language are matters of social convention established by historical processes which shift continually the social prestige of dialect variants.

The obstacles to the acquisition of Standard English sketched by Labov (1964) for American Negro children of certain classes are quite relevant to Creole situations. We must first of all consider the possibility of mechanical constraints upon the linguistic performance of some speakers proceeding from differences in the structure of their vernacular and the structure of prestige pattern. Secondly, there is the likelihood that working and lower-class speakers are not as familiar with the prestige norms as middle-class speakers. Finally, there is the question of conflict of value-systems referred to earlier. On the one hand, Creole situations in islands like Trinidad, Jamaica, etc., are characterized by a striving toward the model provided by Standard British English. This striving has become inseparable from the patterns of upward social mobility to be found in such territories. On the other hand, certain kinds of language skill develop from day to day participation in "social groups in which the appropriate language structure and methods of thinking about self, things and ideas are necessary components of their related styles of group participation" (Cohen 1969: 831). The value-systems thus generated may themselves act to facilitate or impede a person's ability to master the habits associated with other kinds of groups.

Labov (1964) has pointed to the importance of language as a means of identification with friends and members of one's family. He cites evidence that among American Negro teenagers the adolescent peer-group exerts strong pressure against any deviation in the direction of middle-class standard. It seems quite likely that values similar to these may obtain in certain subcultures in Creole communities. We can return to this point later.

We need to judge a child's progress in acquiring new language skills in terms of the norms which exist for the particular language community to which he belongs. Craig (1971: 372) presents the following theoretical model of the language situation characteristic of territories like Jamaica and Trinidad:

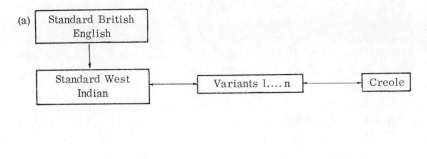

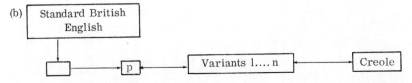

In the second diagram Standard West Indian speech, as accepted in formal social situations, is analyzed into two components; p represents the ways in which such speech differs from Standard British English (Craig 1971: 372).

For pedagogical purposes the relevant aspect of the diagram is the interaction area between Creole and the community's standard. Craig suggests that "at present . . . the spontaneous as well as careful speech of a majority of school age children lies entirely within the interaction area. That is, it is neither Creole nor standard West Indian, nor yet again does it represent a discrete, stable speech norm of its own" (1971: 374). As a result, the Jamaican or Trinidadian child is placed in a language situation in which English is neither a native nor a foreign language. The same is true of other Caribbean islands. The suggestions made by Craig (1972) and Carrington (1971) concerning the sequencing of educational materials in Caribbean communities seem the most promising approach to the teaching of English in these areas. It recognizes that "the population of a given country in the region contains all the likely plateaus in the learner's acquisition of the official language". Since the Creole continuum is essentially a set of layers of increasingly better-learned English super-imposed one on the other, "a set of cuts across the continuum should show a corresponding set of predictable points in the acquisition process' (Carrington 1971: 3–4). The experiments of Craig with school children in Jamaica and Trinidad suggest that the child's learning of English proceeds not in clearly definable steps, but as a gradual process of linguistic change through the "interaction area" of the language continuum.

The approach of Craig and Carrington, though still largely experimental, has offered clear outlines of the kind of work that still needs to be done in the area of language teaching. In the first place, they have emphasized the need for elaborate studies of the Creole continuum and for more sophisticated teaching techniques based on these studies. But they also recognise that this type of work must be supplemented by other kinds of investigation. In particular, there is need for more information on what the teacher knows about the language varieties in use in Creole communities, and especially the varieties used by children in these societies. Part of the aim of the present investigation is to offer a small contribution to this area of our knowledge.

The other aspect of the problem which must be stressed is the likelihood that the child's progress in the acquisition of new language skills is determined to a large extent by the attitudes to language varieties which prevail in the community. Again, relatively little research has been done in this area, and the present article attempts to remedy this situation to some extent by reporting on the attitudes of teachers themselves to the linguistic situation in their community.

The fieldwork for the investigation was carried out in 1970 at two teacher training colleges in Trinidad, the most southerly island of the West Indies. The material for the study consisted of the replies given to a detailed questionnaire by 112 trainee-teachers at these colleges, one located in Port of Spain, the capital of the island, and the other in San Fernando, the second largest town. For the purposes of this study, the respondents have been divided into (a) those who grew up or spent most of their lives in any town area, (b) those who grew up in a country area. Within each of these subgroups, respondents were further divided by ethnic group into Indians and Negroes. It may be worthwhile to point out that within the latter group there were three respondents of mixed (Negro and Indian) parentage. As it turned out, these were the only "mixed" respondents in the entire sample – perhaps surprising in view of the size of the population of persons of mixed blood in the island.[2]

The overall breakdown of the respondents is as follows:

	Town	Country	Total
Indians	30	38	68
Negroes	29	15	44
Total	59	53	112

The following are the figures for each of the teachers' colleges.

(a) Port of Spain	*Town*	*Country*	*Total*
Indians	15	10	25
Negroes	22	10	32
Total	37	20	57

(b) San Fernando	*Town*	*Country*	*Total*
Indians	15	28	43
Negroes	7	5	12
Total	22	33	55

(Five of the 15 Negroes from the "country" in the Port of Spain sample were from Tobago and are not included).

The questionnaire was divided into two sections. The instructions in the Introduction stated that the questions in Section A were aimed "at finding out exactly what things are noticeable as 'good' or 'bad' in the speech of Trinidadians, and also whether the respondent's opinions about speech in Trinidad were the same as those of the people he knew". The questions in Section B were introduced as being of "a more personal nature", aimed at finding out the respondent's opinions about his *own* speech. Respondents were asked to write an essay in reply to this Section, using the questions as a guide.

REPLIES TO SECTION A

Informants were asked to list the things that either they, or other people, as far as they knew, considered to be "bad English" in the speech of Trinidadians.

TABLE I

Linguistic Features Cited as "Bad English"

	No. of Respondents Citing it			
	Port of Spain		San Fernando	
Characteristic	Indians	Negroes	Indians	Negroes
1. Faulty Pronunciation	15	12	29	4
2. Lack of Subject-Verb Agreement	13	14	9	1
3. Use of Words in Wrong Contexts	8	6	11	–

Table I is a list of characteristics singled out by respondents, arranged in order of frequency of citation. (Eight other respondents singled out "bad Grammar" as a characteristic of "bad English", and a number of these specified the lack of Subject-Verb agreement, as being what they had in mind.)

At this point it is well to point out that of the 33 respondents from the country area in the San Fernando sample, 22 singled out "bad Pronunciation" as a characteristic of "bad English". Twenty-one of these were Indians, i.e., 25% of Indians in the sample. This may well bear a significant relationship to the fact that most of these came from small villages in the sugar-belt of the lowlands, where the speech of Indian labourers, etc. is especially singled out for criticism as bad speech, as we shall see.

Other characteristics singled out included:

Characteristic	*Total No. of Respondents Citing it*
Bad Construction of Sentences	11
Reduction of words	9
Use of Slang	12
Wrong use of Pronouns	3
Making up one's own words	5
Use of statements for questions	2
Wrong use of Tense	8
Wrong emphasis on Syllables	4
Use of objective Case as Subject	2

The replies of some respondents to this question often gave the impression that they seized upon, not so much the characteristics more peculiar to Trinidadian speech, but any kind of deviation from Standard English they could think of. The following are examples of this type of feature.

Verbs used wrongly;   Wrong use of adverbs;
Leaving out prepositions;   Wrong use of figurative expressions;
Using adjectives where adverbs should be used.

In fact, three respondents replied to the question with the simple statement that "any deviation from Standard English is considered to be 'bad English'". Furthermore, three Indian respondents from the Country Areas singled out the mixture of Hindi and English in the speech of their parents and older village folk, as being "glaring examples of the rape of the language".

Many informants were more specific in their choice of characteristics of "bad English". These are arranged here under different headings.

Characteristic	*Respondents Citing It*
A. Pronunciation	
"th" Pronounced as "t", "d"	17
Failure to pronounce *-ed* of verbs	5
Failure to pronounce *-ing* of verbs	4
Failure to pronounce *-s* of verbs	4
Using wrong vowel sounds e.g., *OO*, *O* : *wok* for *work*	5
B. "Reduction" of Words. *dong* for *down*, *ley* for *let* *gee* for *give*.	
C. "Fabricated Negatives" – "eh" for "don't", "doesn't"	2
D. Omission of verb "*to be*"	3

Finally, many respondents replied to the question with a list of what they considered to be typical examples of "bad English". The characteristics so far treated have been listed under headings used by the respondents themselves. The following lists of examples (see Table II) are grouped under headings chosen by the investigator.

It would seem from Table II, then, that most of the respondents had a very clear picture of the characteristics of Trinidadian English that could be labelled "bad", "broken", "incorrect", etc., by comparison with whatever model of correctness each had in mind.

At the same time, it seems clear that most respondents were not at all conscious of the fact that the Creole variety of Trinidadian English has its own grammatical system which operates according to different rules from those of Standard English. Informants generally show a great willingness to interpret what are essentially grammatically correct Creole structures as "corruptions" of "good English". The implication of this for educationists is that they are also quite unaware of the real nature of the problem involved in the acquisition of standard language skills by Trinidadian children. This will be borne out in the responses to questions which follow later. As Roger Shuy has suggested in an article on the

TABLE II
Examples of Linguistic Features Cited as "Bad English"

The figures in parenthesis indicate the number of respondents citing each feature.

Particular Examples Listed

A. Consonantal and Vocalic Features

dis, dat, dem, dey, etc. (7)
carh, kyah, etc. for *can't* (9)
gal, gyul for *girl*; (3) *dutty* for
dirty (2)
wahta for *"water",* * *wah* for *want* *

B. Reduction of Words

wey for *where, dey* for *there* (14)
gee, gi for *give* * (6)
leh for *let* (7)
whey, wha for *what* (3)
dong for *down* (3)

C. Pronouns

(a) Use of "Nominative" for
"Objective" Forms
leh we go, leh she go, etc. (11)
He ent like she; Gi she one
You think he go send we : (5)

(b) Use of "objective" form in
Subject Position
me eh going : (6)

(c) Use of *all-yuh* for *You* (plur.) (1)

D. Demonstratives

Dem people, *dem* boys, etc. (2)

E. Possessive pronouns. (9)

me belly; *you* friend
gee de girl she mango
my one better than he one

Grammatical Features

(1) *Use of "eh" as Negative* (15)
E.g., I eh going down dey
     Me eh know

(2) *Use of "does" plus verb* (6)
E.g., I does work in the garment factory.
     We does eat peas

(3) *"Omission" of verb "To be"* (11)
She too stupid
My one better dan he one
She day day outside

(4) *Use of "go" instead of "will"* (12)
You tink he go send we
An go see you

(5) *Subject-Verb Agreement* (21)
I is a boss; I is in the bedroom
Tom have; You is

(6) *Hypercorrections* (6)
We knows two songs
They does; Where do you lives.

(7) *Lack of Inversion in Questions* (3)
E.g., You is a teacher?
     You tink he go send we?

(8) *Miscellaneous* (6)
Is what happen now?
He dresses good.
Way yuh name? Ah name Tom.
Ah spree for so!
Gi' meh ah chance
He is a big man

(9) *Use of "de" as past-tense marker* (2)
E.g., *Ah de hear* [3]

Vocabulary Items

E.g., *oukou* for *roucou*
     hammick for *hammock*
     breakfast for *lunch*
     tea for *tea, coffee, chocolate,* etc. [4]

---

* All of these forms were listed only by Indian respondents from Country areas.

problems of language development among disadvantaged American children, "it is no difficult matter to say that the current linguistic sophistication of teachers is rather limited" (Shuy 1970: 125).

OPINIONS ON TOWN/COUNTRY SPEECH DIFFERENCES

Section A of the questionnaire also contained a series of questions aimed at finding out the extent of consciousness among respondents of speech differences between people living in town areas and those living in country areas. An introductory question asked whether the speech of West Indians from other islands was different from Trinidadian speech, and in what ways. Most of the respondents, it turned out, were familiar with other West Indians in Trinidad. The 97 respondents who replied to this question all agreed that there were differences, and of these, 86 singled out pronunciation and "accent" as the chief distinguishing features. Only 6 chose to mention differences in grammar, whilst 8 mentioned the use of different "slang" expressions and 3 mentioned the slower rate of speech of other West Indians as compared with Trinidadians.

If nothing else, the responses to this question established that there was a strong awareness of speech and speech differences among respondents. In reply to the question whether they thought Trinidadian speech to be better or worse than that of other West Indians, 40 said Trinidadian speech was better, 33 recognized the differences but offered no value judgment, 2 thought that all West Indian speech was just as bad, 2 found the speech of other West Indians amusing, and 23 thought that the speech of other West Indians was better, 13 of them singling out Barbadian speech in particular as being better than Trinidadian speech.

The group of questions aimed at finding out respondents' awareness of town/country speech differences in Trinidad itself was roughly as follows:

(1) Did they think that country people spoke differently from town people?
(2) What did they think of the speech of people in their community?
(3) Did people from the town or country as the case might be, recognise where they came from by their speech?
(4) Did they think people in the town or country as the case might be, liked the speech they used?

Of the 99 respondents replying to the first question, 96 agreed that there were differences. Thirty-one specified pronunciation as the chief distinguishing factor, 9 mentioned the greater use of slang in country areas, 24 simply mentioned that country people used "more broken English", more "dialect", or different "grammar". Two respondents mentioned the mixture of Hindi and English peculiar to the speech of older Indian people in their country communities. No direct question was asked about the relative merits of country and town speech, and on the whole most respondents offered no value judgments. Yet a number of respondents used terms like "less refined" (5), and "less correct" or simply "worse" (12).

But in response to Question (2) above, respondents were more prepared to offer judgment on the speech of people in their own communities. The following table gives a breakdown of their replies.

TABLE III

Comments by Respondents on the English Used in Their Own Communities

| | "Fair to Good" | | "Bad" | | Non-committal | |
	P.O.S.	San F'do	P.O.S.	San F'do	P.O.S.	San F'do
Town						
Indians	5	5	1	4	0	1
Negroes	14	6	4	2	0	0
Country						
Indians	1	4	4	16	0	0
Negroes	0	0	1	2	3	1

Among the non-responses were 5 of the 10 Indians from the country area in the Port of Spain sample, and 5 of the 10 Negroes from the country area, including two from Tobago. Though only 76 respondents replied to this question, there seems to be a marked contrast between respondents living in town and country areas in their judgment of the speech of people in their community. Thus only 5 in all from the country claimed that the speech in their community was "good", while 23 from the country including 16 of the 28 Indians in the San Fernando sample, characterized the speech in their community as "bad". By contrast, among town respondents, only 11 characterized the speech of their community as "bad", while 30 considered it to be "fair to good".

Many respondents seemed to have misunderstood Question (3) above, which sought to find out whether respondents from the country would be recognized by town people as belonging to the country, and vice-versa. Only the answers of those who seemed to have understood the question are included here. In all 26 respondents from the town stated that people recognized them as being town-dwellers by their speech. Twenty-six answered in the negative, and a few others said they never gave it any thought. Among respondents from the country, 20 agreed that people recognized them as country-dwellers by their speech, whilst 24 did not think so, and a few had either not given it any thought, or felt that it was unimportant. One Indian country respondent mentioned that he varied his speech in the town, so that people could not tell where he was from, whilst another said that town people used to recognize him as a country-dweller by his speech, but no longer did so.

Question (4) above, sought to determine the attitudes of people of the town and country, respectively, to the speech of respondents. Most respondents said that their speech was well liked in their own communities, but offered no comment on attitudes to their speech in other communities (non-rural, or non-urban, as the case might be). In the Port of Spain sample, only 1 respondent claimed that his speech was not liked, giving no reason for this, whilst in the San Fernando sample all said that their speech was well liked. It was in the responses to this question that the first general comments on the use of varieties of English by respondents began to appear. A few respondents pointed out that acceptance of their speech depended on the variety they chose, and the people they spoke to, and said that they varied their speech accordingly. In a few cases, there was a marked difference between town and country respondents. Five of the latter (all Indians) said that their speech was disliked by people in the towns. And a number of other country respondents took the opportunity to comment, for example, on towns people's "attempt to show an air of superiority by use of supposedly better language". Another respondent wrote:

The expression of town people is polluted with false airs; Country folk are loose in expression (Negro from Port of Spain).

Some respondents thought town speech more "correct";

People in the country have their own dialect but people in the town are all mixed and because of regular opportunities for listening to good speech, speak correctly (Indian from Town).

Some respondents were more precise in their evaluation of the reasons for town/country differences, which they attributed to education, occupational opportunity, social status and so on.

All important positions and offices are in the towns. People are more aware of the use of speaking correctly and they come in contact regularly with educated and intelligent people.

Common to most replies, then, is the acknowledgment that there *are* speech differences between town and country, and that generally these are the differences between more, and less, "correct" speech. After this point, respondents are divided on the issue of the values to be attached to such differences of speech behaviour. This is complicated by their recognition of similar differences among some people of country areas (by education and social status) no less than among townsfolk. Though there *is* disagreement among respondents as to the desirability or otherwise of such differences, their views at least have in common the recognition of a *general* difference in values which is expressed as follows by a Negro respondent from the country:

Up to a point I affirm this view (that country speech is different from town speech). But this is so only insofar as country people approach life differently from town people. The whole setting in rural districts is quite different from a town. Thus things are likely to be expressed in somewhat different terms.

Summary

The responses to the questions in Section A clearly indicate at least one thing – that there is a great deal of awareness on the part of these respondents, of the varieties of English used in their island, and of the particular characteristics which distinguish one variety from another. Furthermore, there is a great deal of agreement on the identification of the "less correct" variety with country areas, and the "more correct" with town areas. More detailed comments on these differences, and more subjective evaluation of their role in speech behaviour, are the concern of Section B of the questionnaire.

Responses to Section B

As already mentioned, the questions in Section B were introduced to respondents as "aimed at finding out their opinions of their own speech". As a preliminary, they were asked to provide an idea of language(s) other than "English" used by their parents. Among all Indian respondents, there were 53 whose parents used "Hindi" at home, 33 of these were from the country, and 20 from the town. Eleven of the country respondents had a working command of Hindi, 7 only understood it, having acquired a small vocabulary as well. Of the town respondents, 8 had a command of Hindi, and 3 only understood it to some extent. Of all 29 informants who had either an active or passive command of Hindi, 17 were from the San Fernando sample, and 12 from the Port of Spain sample. Among all Negro respondents, there were 14 whose parents spoke Creole French, and one whose parents spoke "Spanish". Half of these (7) were living in Port of Spain, and of these 5 had a "passive" command of Patois, and none could speak it, except for a few words and phrases. Only one other respondent (living in San Fernando) had a command of Patois. whilst another (from the country) had a command of Spanish.

Question Set "A": To determine the types of attitudes they had to their own use of English, respondents were asked a series of questions about:

(a) Whether they considered their speech to be good or bad.
(b) Whether they had ever tried to change their speech.
(c) Whether they had received encouragement from parents or teachers to improve their speech.
(d) Whether they had ever felt embarrassed at being unable to speak "correct English".

A total of 48 respondents stated that they had no trouble in speaking correct English, whilst 37 said that they had, either as a general rule, or sometimes. By far the largest group of those reporting difficulties of this nature consisted of Indian respondents from the country areas. Seventeen of the 28 Indian respondents from the country in the San Fernando sample reported such difficulty, 3 of them qualifying it with "sometimes only". By contrast, only 5 of the 15 town respondents in the same sample said that they had difficulties, 4 of them qualifying the statement with "sometimes only". Of the 15 Indians from the town in the Port of Spain sample, only 4 reported difficulty with "correct English". The number of Negro informants from the country areas is perhaps too small to make any generalizations worthwhile, but in both samples, there was a greater percentage of country respondents who reported having difficulties with "correct English". However, all 5 of the Negroes from Tobago in the Port of Spain sample said that they had no difficulty.

Almost all respondents had received, as children, stong encouragement from their teachers to "improve" their speech. Again the features to be "improved" included pronunciation, verb-subject agreement, etc. By contrast, 43 respondents reported that they had received little or no

encouragement from their parents to improve their speech, whilst only 40
reported such encouragement. A further 10 pointed out that there had
been no need for their parents (or teachers) to "correct" their speech,
since they attempted to do that of their own accord. In all, 47 respondents
said that they had tried to improve their speech at one time or another,
whilst 32 said they had not. Nine others said they thought of their speech
as acceptable "Trinidadian", but stated that there were some occasions
on which they would attempt to improve it. It is likely that many such
attempts at improving speech were prompted, not by the encouragement
of parents, but by respondents' own desires. Therefore the affirmative
replies to the last two questions, (b) and (c) respectively, do not necessarily coincide in all cases.

Closely connected with question (a) above, was question (d), which
asked whether respondents had ever felt embarrassed at their inability to
speak "correct English". "Yes" responses to this totalled only 19, including 2 who reported being embarrassed only in the presence of foreigners.
Thirty-eight respondents said they had never felt embarrassed in a situation that called for "correct English", whilst 3 pointed out that such a
situation had never arisen with them. In all, then, only 60 of the 112
respondents replied to this question, so it is difficult to make any
comparison with other responses, except to point out that there is a size-
able discrepancy between the numbers who reported difficulty with
"correct English", and those who reported embarrassment due to their
lack of a command of correct English. This, of course, is not surprising if
we accept that, even in formal situations involving speakers of "correct
English", demands on language skills need not be very pronounced;
furthermore, the ideal "standard of correctness" which respondents felt
unable to attain, may be far in excess of the actual "standard of correctness" acceptable in such situations.

SOME TOWN/COUNTRY AND INDIAN/NEGRO DIFFERENCES

As in the case of previous questions, there are a number of noticeable
differences between certain groups of respondents, in their replies to this
set of questions. The percentage of Indians from country areas who reported having attempted to improve or change their speech was by far the
highest for any group of respondents – 18 of the 28 in the San Fernando
sample, and 5 of the 10 in the Port of Spain sample. Among Town
Indians, 15 of the 30 in both samples reported such attempts (7 in Port of

Spain; 8 in San Fernando). A far smaller percentage of Negroes reported similar attempts – only 13 of the 44 from both town and country in both samples. Eight of the 15 Negroes from country areas were among these 13, and only 5 of the 29 from the town areas.

Thus there seems to be a marked Town/Country difference for both ethnic groups, and a marked Indian/Negro difference for town as well as country areas. In both town and country, a far greater percentage of Indians than of Negroes report themselves as attempting to improve their speech.

Similar differences are to be found in the reports of encouragement from parents for respondents to improve their speech. A higher percentage of Negro respondents in both town and country areas stated that they had received such encouragement. For both Negro and Indian respondents, a higher percentage of parents offered encouragement in town areas than in country areas. And again, the most noticeable group in this case were the Indian respondents from country areas. Eight of the 10 in the Port of Spain sample, and 14 of the 28 in the San Fernando sample, reported no encouragement from their parents, and of these, 7 went on to point out that their parents couldn't encourage them to speak "correct English" when they themselves did not know what "correct English" meant.

For country respondents, and particularly for the Indians among them, attempts to change speech are reported as frequently as lack of encouragement from parents. We might interpret these facts as reflections of the stigmas attached to country Indian speech, of which the speech of the older country folk must be particularly representative. The lack of encouragement from parents (many of whom did not know what "correct English" was) and the spontaneous attempts by respondents to improve their speech, can then be viewed as consequences of the same situation.

"Domains" of language use

Question Set "B": As we saw in the case of certain questions in Section A, even when not directly asked about their use of language, many respondents felt obliged to point out that their use of either "broken" or "correct" English depended on various external factors. A series of questions in Section B was designed to elicit information about the factors influencing choice of one or the other variety of English. In the first place, informants were asked whether they would use "Trinidadian" or "correct

English" in a variety of situations. Almost all reported that they would use "correct English" in the following situations:

(a)   When at work (as teachers)   (b)   In Church.

Only 6 said that they used Trinidadian when at work, and 12 when at church. A further 7 claimed to use both Trinidadian and correct English when at work, and 9 when in church. At the other extreme, almost all agreed that they would use Trinidadian in the following situations:

(a)   When telling a really funny joke.
(b)   When quarrelling.
(c)   When "liming" or playing cards.
For (a)   only 2 respondents said they used "correct English".
For (b)   4 used English, and 6 used both Trinidadian and English.
For (c)   6 used English, and 7 used both Trinidadian and English.

For the above situations, there was not any obvious distinction between respondents from town or country, or between Indians and Negroes, though it may be worthwhile to point out that of the 13 respondents who said they used Trinidadian some times when at work, 11 were from town areas (6 Negroes and 5 Indians).

There was a third set of situations for which there was far less agreement on which variety of English was used by respondents (or to them). These included,

(a)   When talking to their parents.
(b)   When their parents spoke to them.
(c)   When with friends around home.

In each of these cases, a substantial majority stated that only Trinidadian was used. But 21 respondents reported using English to their parents, whilst 7 used both Trinidadian and English. Eighteen respondents reported that their parents used "correct English" when speaking to them, and the parents of 4 used both Trinidadian and English. Finally, when speaking with friends around home, 14 respondents used "correct English", and 11 used both. There was no striking difference between town and country respondents in their reports of the use of English in any of the above situations. However, in two cases, (a) and (c), the number of Indians who reported the use of correct English was noticeably higher than that of Negroes. This is presented in the following Table.

TABLE IV

Number of Indian and Negro Respondents Reporting
Use of "Correct English" in Three Settings

	Indians	Negroes
Telling a joke	14	7
"Liming"	18	7
Quarrelling	10	8

Of course, in the light of the relative total numbers of Indians and Negroes in the sample of respondents (68 Indians to 44 Negroes) such differences may not be significant at all. At any rate what we have are three sets of situations distinguished from each other by the extent of agreement among respondents as to what type of language is used by them in each. There are two situations in which almost all would use English, 3 in which almost all would use Trinidadianese and 2 in which, though most would use Trinidadianese, a substantial minority would choose to use "correct English". This at least argues once more for a significant awareness among respondents of the varieties of language at their command, and their propriety in various situations.

Values attached to varieties

Another series of questions was designed to find out from respondents their own feelings about the values attached to the varieties of English in use in their community.

Question Set "C": They were asked:

(1) Whether Trinidadianese was their most natural way of speaking.
(2) Whether there were times when they had to use it.
(3) Whether their friends were annoyed at their use of "correct English" to them.
(4) Whether people ever annoyed them by speaking "correctly".

Respondents were left free to make their own comments in reply to these questions, which did not demand simple yes-no responses. Consequently a perhaps more accurate picture of their attitudes to the language varities emerged. Surprisingly, in response to the first question, though a

majority of respondents (51) said that Trinidadianese was their most
natural medium of speaking, 20 respondents commented instead that they
preferred to use "correct English", and another 4 reported that for them
English, not Trinidadianese, was the most natural way of speaking.
Moreover, 9 others pointed out that Trinidadianese was proper at times,
but English was also required very often. Twenty-eight respondents
chose not to respond to this question. There were few responses to the
second question as to whether Trinidadianese was compulsory at times,
though of those who replied most agreed that it would be required at
some time or another, either among friends, or with certain people. A
frequent comment was that very often in speaking to persons of a "lower-
status" than themselves, respondents would have to use Trinidadianese
if only to make themselves understood. The third question sought to
elicit more details about the propriety of Trinidadianese in particular
with respondents' friends. Table V gives the breakdown of responses to
this question. The figures represent the number of persons giving each
reply.

TABLE V

Replies of Respondents to Question (3) Set (C)

"Yes"	"Sometimes"	"No"	No Response
17	11	23	59

A total of 64 respondents answered question (4) above. Of these only 4
reported being annoyed at the use of "correct English" as a general rule.
Thirty said that they were never annoyed at the use of correct English,
many adding that, on the contrary, they admired it, and one stating his
annoyance, not at English, but at Trinidadianese. The remaining 30
admitted being annoyed with persons whose correct English was
"affected", particularly those who insisted on adopting a "foreign"
accent when speaking "correct English". Other respondents reported
feeling embarrassed when some people attempted to use "correct
English" and displayed a limited capacity for it.

A note on rural Indians: Though the failure of so many respondents to
reply to the above questions makes it unwise to draw final conclusions, a
few points are worth mentioning. The first is that of those who, in reply to
question (1) above, emphasized their preference for "correct English"

rather than Trinidadianese, by far the largest group consisted of Indian respondents from the San Fernando sample: (17 out of the total of 43). Of these, 11 were from country areas, and 6 from the town. This situation may be compared with that noted earlier, under the discussion of replies to question Set A for the group of Indian respondents from rural areas. Thus the same group that distinguished itself from the others by (a) reporting difficulty with "correct English", and (b) reporting serious efforts to improve their speech, is now distinguished by the admission of a preference for "correct English" rather than Trinidadianese as their normal means of communication. But the lack of a full response to these questions forbids any conclusions to be drawn. Furthermore, this preference for "correct English" is by no means general among the Indians from the country who replied.

Comment: What emerges from the replies to the questions in Sets B and C above is the lack of any generally accepted standard of propriety for either of the two varieties of English. Respondents do not agree unanimously in their replies to any of the questions. The greatest degree of agreement is in their reports of usage of English and Trinidadianese respectively for certain situations (Question Set B). This agreement is even less in the case of Question Set C, where no clear pattern of values emerges. Generally we seem to have a number who regard Trinidadianese as either completely unacceptable, or at best a necessary evil, another group who accept both Trinidadianese and English as being proper in particular circumstances, and finally a third group (a minority) who acknowledge with reluctance the need for correct English in many situations, and are highly critical of the stigmas attached to Trinidadianese. Similarly, though the group of country Indians can be singled out as distinct from the others in their replies to various questions, there is no generally clear pattern of distinctions either between town and country, or between one ethnic group and the other.

By way of elaborating these points, we may first of all consider the replies of respondents to a set of questions designed to obtain an idea of their attitude to Trinidadianese itself. Respondents were asked:

Question Set "D":

(1) Whether they thought Trinidadian "slang" added vigour to the speech of Trinidadians, and whether it ought to be discouraged.
(2) What they thought of the use of Trinidadianese in literature.

(3) What they thought of the use of Trinidadianese in certain articles in the newspapers and in certain advertisements over the radio.
(4) Whether they thought teachers should use Trinidadianese to assist in explaining things in class.
(5) Whether they thought Trinidadianese should be taught instead of English.

Table VI gives the breakdown of replies to Question (1).

TABLE VI

Replies of Respondents to Question (1) (Set D)

(The Use of Trinidadian Slang)	
"Should be Discouraged"	"Add vigour to the language"
31	76

Of the 31 who thought slang expressions should be discouraged, 24 were Indians, 16 of them from country areas. For question 2 and 3, by far the greatest number of respondents felt that Trinidadianese was appropriate in the novels and plays with which they were familiar, and was also effective in newspapers and in advertisements.
Table VII gives the breakdown of replies to question (2).

TABLE VII

Replies of Respondents to Question (2) (Set D)

(The Use of Trinidadianese in Novels and Plays)		
"Appropriate"	"Humourous"	"Undesirable"
83	8	17

The breakdown of replies to question (3) is presented in Table VIII.

TABLE VIII

Replies of Respondents to Question (3) (Set D)

(The Use of Trinidadianese in the Mass Media)		
"Appropriate"	"Humourous"	"Undesirable"
89	6	12

Of the 61 respondents who replied to question (4), 39 thought it a good idea to use Trinidadianese to assist in teaching, many of them adding that they had in fact found it extremely helpful in their own classes in primary schools. The other 22 were opposed to any use of Trinidadianese in class. Finally, only 53 respondents replied to question (5) and of these all but 10 were opposed to the idea of introducing Trinidadianese to replace English as a subject to be taught. Of these 10, only 2 thought Trinidadianese should replace English, and the other eight thought that both should be taught.

In the responses to this set of questions then, we once more find no unanimously held set of values about the language of Trinidadians. The hostility of a few to Trinidadianese is matched by the hostility of a few to "correct English".

The majority of respondents, while seeming to accept both, waver in their views on the appropriateness of each, and on the relative values to be attached to each in various situations and for different purposes. A typical statement by one of those hostile to Trinidadianese is the following reply by a country Indian to question (5).

This is all bush. English was borrowed from the Englishman and as such we owe an obligation to preserve it.

Also typical of a few is the following comment by an Indian from the town.

Personally, I believe it could be quite a laudable feat to change from "correct English" to Trinidadianese in our society. Should this system be accepted, we could be better able to communicate with each other, and many complexes will be displaced.

And in between are various comments which seek to point out the respective merits of each variety of English. The following are examples:

(1) Trinidadianese is a unique and colourful dialect and serves to illustrate more fully the desired idea. For example Sparrow's "a gi she arreddy" serves the imagination better and communicates better than "I gave her already". (Town Indian)

(2) There are times when one should use correct English, but one should know the time and place for doing so. (Town Negro)

This middle ground is occupied by the vast majority of the respondents, even though they may not agree absolutely on the "time and place for doing so". And with these, there is always, in the background the sense of a very clear appreciation of the merits of each variety of English. For some respondents for instance, advertisements in Trinidadianese are not merely desirable, but desirable because they appeal to what people feel most at home with, and "newspaper articles like "MACAW" are quite in order as they remove from the people that feeling of self-consciousness and guilt at not using the "Queen's English". And not far removed from this is the readiness to show up any pretence on the part of those who abuse the balance between the two varieties:

Some people on the other hand try to speak correct English and make very horrible and silly mistakes; for example there is a man who always says *wather* for *water* and *daughther* for *daughter*. Another one, a big elderly lady working for the government says *I has*, when *you comes*, *I sees*, and this is contrived all the time. (Country Indian)

Social values: Such comments obviously invite a more extended consideration of the views of respondents on the role of the 2 varieties of English in Trinidadian society. Three of the questions put to respondents are relevant here:

Question Set "E":
(1)   What did they think of the Prime Minister's Speech, and would they choose any other politician's as being better?
(2)   Could they comment on particular (groups of) Trinidadians whose speech they considered either good or bad?
(3)   Would they use English or Trinidadianese when being interviewed for a job, and why?

All but 20 respondents professed themselves impressed with the speech of the Prime Minister, but the real interest was in the alternatives that these 20, as well as some who admired the P.M.'s speech, offered as being good exponents of "good English". Thirty-eight respondents chose other members of Parliament, in most cases specifying them by name. In response to the second question, politicians were chosen by 27 respondents as being persons who spoke good English. Radio announcers were chosen by 7 respondents. Other choices of speakers of good English included teachers (3), students (1), office workers (1), persons of the "upper income bracket" (2), educated persons (1), "middle-class people" (1), and salesmen (1). Again in many cases particular persons were mentioned by name as being fine speakers of English. Very few respondents chose to pick on persons whose speech they considered poor, but their choices included: Country people (5); canefield workers (2); labourers on the road (2); uneducated country people (1); older people in sugar-cane areas (1); Indians in rural areas (1); the children of

East Indian parents from India (1); "uneducated and lower-class persons" (1); older country people, and young country people who pay no attention to speech (1). Certain respondents mentioned particular persons by name, among them (to complicate things) a certain Indian M.P. and no less than the Prime Minister, who in one respondent's view, was too fond of gutter language like "moko jumbie"; "get the hell outa here"; and "the bloomin' church".

The above choices reflect very well the comments made in responses to other parts of the questionnaire, where in fact no direct questions on the role of language as a marker of social status were put. Thus, in response to questions about town/country speech differences, many comments of this nature were made. Similar awareness of the social significance of language emerged in the replies to the 3rd question above. All but one respondent agreed that they would have to use Standard English when being interviewed for a job, and many of them pointed out that this was essential if they were to make any impression on their interviewers as being qualified for the job. In the essays written in response to Section B of the questionnaire, many comments were made on the correlation between occupation, or status, and language. The following are typical:

I believe that Trinidadianese is a natural dialect which everyone enjoys. It is only when one gets into the so-called "social" groups that one finds there is special emphasis on "good English". (Town Negro)

In fact speech correction is something unexpected in a home where there is a farmer, motor-mechanic, chauffeur or labourer. (Country Indian)

There is evidently considerable awareness among respondents of such correlations between "correct" English and social "status".

Finally we may consider some of the comments made by respondents concerning their own use of the varieties of English in various situations, involving friends and other participants.

A SKETCH OF LANGUAGE CHOICE BY RESPONDENTS

The following assessment is based roughly on Herman's (1961) discussion of the possibility of using the choice of language as a behavioural index to group preferences and to the direction of social adjustment. Herman attends first of all to the developmental pattern of language usage, and divides the adjustment period in acquiring a new language (skill) into

five categories beginning with anticipatory socialisation and ending with
the integration of the new language skill into the total life situation.
Such details need not concern us here, since it is at any rate impossible to
draw conclusions of any great accuracy from the replies to a questionnaire.
However, many replies do give some insight into respondent's adjustment
to the language situation with which they were confronted at one stage or
another of their lives. The following replies give an idea of the kinds of
reaction that occurred:

(1)   When I started school at the age of 5, I discovered that there were different ways of
      expressing some of the things we said at home, so I tried to change my speech to a
      better form of English. (Town Indian)

(2)   (When I went to school) at times I felt embarrassed when I had to speak with the
      better-speaking children from the town, because I had difficulty to express myself
      like them. I was quite conscious of this fact and I tried to improve my speech by
      listening to intelligent people converse and reading short stories. (Country Indian)

(3)   As soon as I came of age and had done English to some fair degree, I tried to change
      my manner of speech and use Standard English as much as possible. – I was never
      embarrassed for lack of proper speech and sometimes I feel disappointed when I do
      not hear persons speak properly. (Town Negro)

(4)   I have tried to change my speech at College. This was simply because my accent was
      bad – typical country chap. In fact, I introduced a programme of correct speech at
      home so that my brothers and sisters spoke well. This soon rubbed off on my parents.
      (Country Indian)

The above responses represent what seems to be the general pattern
among respondents, but as in so many other cases discussed earlier there
are exceptions like the following comments:

(1)   I have tried to change my speech but find the effort disgusting and hypocritical. (Town
      Negro)

And the pattern is completely reversed for one of the respondents who
reports as follows:

(2)   I grew up in an English-speaking home and I was always encouraged to speak "proper
      English". At the convent where I received my education, the emphasis was always on
      good English. Because of this I always found it comparatively easy to speak good
      English. After leaving school I tried to change my language to the more local form,
      because I was always ridiculed for my "correct speech." (Town Indian)

Keeping in mind this picture of adjustment to the two varieties of English
by respondents, we can now consider the factors influencing their use in

different settings. Herman distinguishes three major sources of influence: (a) personal needs, (b) the immediate situation, (c) the background situation. He concludes that the speaker with a choice between two languages is a person in an overlapping situation, i.e., he is located in the common part of two psychological situations that exist simultaneously for him. Hence:

(1) The possibility of conflict between personal needs and group demands.
(2) The problem of how the background of a situation influences behaviour in an immediate situation.

Herman discusses in some detail the conditions under which each of these factors gains in salience. Again the nature of our material makes it unwise to attempt too close a classification along Herman's lines, but it still allows us to trace certain obvious and general tendencies toward language choice by the respondents.

CASES WHERE THE BACKGROUND SITUATION IS DOMINANT

According to Hunt (1966), this category refers primarily either to role behaviour or to language domains ("areas of interaction . . . in which the usage of a particular language is customary") (Hunt 1966: 243).

(a) *Language domains:*

(1) Speaking Trinidadianese in our environment is unique. It fits in with a good "lime" and "fete" when people like to "ole talk" a lot. A calypso in good English would sound very corny and out of place. It would lose its significance. (Town Indian)

(2) Trinidadianese is used also among the upper-class-bracket people especially when sharing in jokes or other special occasions. This may be done merely for relaxation and comfort. (Town Indian)

Earlier we mentioned other language domains in which either Trinidadianese or "correct English" was felt to be more appropriate.

(b) *When language usage means group identification and acceptance:*
Cases involved here include both those in which the natural preference of the speaker is for Trinidadianese, and those in which it is for correct English. In either case, there are times when personal needs must give

way to the demands of the situation, as well as those in which the forces
arising from the two influences point to the use of the same language.

Preference for Trinidadianese

(1)   My friends would not be annoyed if I spoke too correctly to them. It is just that I feel
      that the Trinidadianese helps in bringing us closer together. (Country Negro)

(2)   Bad English is a natural way of talking for very often when one endeavours to speak
      good English one is laughed at by friends.

Preference for Trinidadianese leading to conflict

There are some of my friends who disapprove of Trinidadianese. They feel it is beneath
their dignity. I don't think that way. (Country Indian)

Many people regard you as a type of freak if you attempt to speak correct English, and you
are in turn humiliated in Trinidadian.

The tendency with me is to use broken English with those who customarily use this type
and to revert to formal English at other occasions. This change follows naturally with
change in mood and situation without much conscious thought. (Town Indian)

Preference for English leading to conflict
In one case, a respondent (mentioned earlier) who had always been used
to speaking "correct English", finds this preference in conflict with the
demands of her friends:

After leaving school I tried to change my language to the more local form, because I was
always ridiculed for my "correct speech"... . I still find it difficult either to comprehend
or to speak Trinidadianese. New acquaintances find my speech irksome, but old friends
accept me for what I am. (Town Indian)

(c)   *When the speaker wishes to be identified as from a particular group
      or to be dissociated from it:*
It is difficult in the case of many responses to distinguish this factor from
the one preceding. Very often language choice is determined simultaneously by a desire to gain acceptance, and a desire to be dissociated from
a particular group – particularly when it means being considered "affected" or hypocritical:

There are times when one has to use Trinidadianese. For if you were to try to speak proper
English to the ordinary man in the street he would think you were trying to "play white",
and again if you tried this correct English act with your friends they would probably
leave you out of their affairs, for they would say you were "high falutin". (Town Negro)

A great number of respondents reported this reaction among addressees to be spoken to in correct English. As we saw earlier, even those who in principle favoured the use of "correct English" over Trinidadianese often declared themselves annoyed or embarrassed by efforts at "correct" speech that were overdone. In the country areas in particular, there seems to be a strong awareness of the artificiality of "over-correct" speech, as evidenced by the number of respondents who stated that to speak correctly to villagers was to invite accusations of "being from England" or "being white". The following comments may be fairly representative:

(1) I will never forget the time when after spending two years in England a villager tried to speak differently. The people felt that he was showing off. I think that plain, simple, straightforward English is what is necessary. (Country Indian)

(2) Since most of my friends are persons who have a fairly good English education, I do not think that they will be annoyed if you spoke too correctly to them. Yet if the listeners realize that I'm making a special effort which does not come naturally, they will be annoyed. (Country Negro)

Similarly, there were many cases reported by respondents where it was they who were being assigned to a category from which they wished to be associated, by friends who chose to address them correctly.

Sometimes friends who think I am more educated than they annoy me by trying to speak too correctly. (Country Negro)

And vice-versa,

Trinidadianese is the most natural way of talking for a Trinidadian and is most useful in bringing about a feeling of comradeship especially when trying to communicate with persons who might consider themselves to be beneath your social status, and have a tendency to be withdrawn and anti-social. In such cases the persons would be annoyed if you tried to be "too English" with them. (Town Negro)

(d) *Personal needs dominant:*
There are many incidents reported by respondents in which they felt embarrassed because they were unable to speak correct English. Similar cases are not grouped together by Hunt (1966) but treated under such diverse headings as:

(a) When the speaker wishes to be identified as from a particular group or to be dissociated from it (Background Situation Dominant).

(b)   When the situation provokes high tension (Personal Needs Dominant).
(c)   When language skills are inadequate for language usage best fitted to the social situation.

Once more it is very difficult to isolate factors as precisely as one would like. Indeed, it is not unlikely that in most cases it is impossible to draw distinctions between one such influence and another. All of the above influences seem to be operating on language choice (often the choice of silence) in such cases as the following:

There was an occasion on which, though I never felt embarrassed, I kept my mouth shut. This was an occasion when a young university graduate was showing off on his return home. Naturally there were other "grades" and the topics and words went sky high. (Town Negro)

I had a very embarrassing experience when I happened to be among some friends whom I met at a party. They were of a different social standing – doctors to be quite truthful – and I did not say much. In fact I took the least part in the conversation for fear of saying the wrong things. (Country Indian)

(e)   *Influence of immediate situation:*
Hunt (1966: 252) rightly points out that this category is difficult to differentiate from the two immediately preceding, "since it overlaps with both role behaviour and language fluency". He concludes that it may refer to "specific existential situations rather than to socially established customs of language usage". In such cases, factors of custom or language fluency enter in, but the language decision is determined primarily by other factors. The following seem to be good examples:

Whenever I meet people less educated than myself I have to modify my speech to enable them to understand fully what I'm saying. (Town Negro)

At times it is necessary to speak in this way (Trinidadianese) so that persons who might not have had a sound English education might understand you.

Perhaps it is in the middle ground of all these factors that we must look for those influences that are most general among the respondents. Most of them seem to accept (as we have previously pointed out) that the two linguistic varieties have each its own propriety and acceptability. For them it seems possible to employ both without developing phobias about the relative merits of each, or complexes about the priority of one over the other:

I have become accustomed to both local English and standard English which to some people are like two languages. (Country Indian)

I can shift freely from Trinidadian to good English, and this helps with the different friends I have. . . . (Town Negro)

There are times when one has to use Trinidadianese . . . and there are times when one should use correct English. But one should know the time and place for doing so. (Town Negro)

It is to be hoped that the results of this investigation will go some way toward filling the substantial gap that exists in our knowledge of factors governing the use of language varieties in Creole communities. The investigation itself, of course, is only a small beginning. From both a general sociolinguistic point of view, and for educational purposes, there is need for more research on the functional distribution of language varieties in creole situations. We need to investigate the attitudes, values and motivations concerning linguistic subsystems, their features and their uses. A variety of factors is involved. Some concern "the variety of genre – narration, dance, drama, song, instrumental music, etc. – that interrelate with speech in the communicative life of the society." (Hymes 1968: 12). Other factors involved include contexts of situation defined by the relationship between participants, and their social roles in the community.

In Creole societies we also need to investigate the attitudes which exist among various social groups toward the varieties of linguistic behaviour in their communities. For instance, Alleyne (1961) suggests that there are two important sections of St. Lucian society, defined primarily by their group attitude toward Creole French. Adherence to this attitude cuts across social divisions based on traditional criteria such as birth, wealth and education. Such attitudes can lead to great changes in linguistic usage, particularly in societies where the former dominance of colonial powers has been removed. Berry (1961) has pointed to the positive attitudes toward Creole English (Krio) developing among Sierra Leone creoles:

On the one hand, it (English) is the model language, the language of social and cultural prestige. On the other hand . . . the need is keenly felt at times to assert the individuality of Krio by emphasizing differences from standard English wherever possible (Berry 1961:3).

It seems likely that such ambivalence is characteristic of many Caribbean creole speakers who may wish to adapt their behaviour to the culturally and socially more prestigious norm, yet still wish to preserve something of a separate identity by using the creole variety. It would be interesting to see whether the strength of such attitudes varied from one social group to the next in these Caribbean communities.[5]

From the point of view of the educationist, at least one significant possibility has emerged from the present investigation: that the social values attached to varieties of English in Creole Communities must be regarded as substantially different from those which obtain in more usual dialect situations. Thus Carrington is justified in questioning, for creole situations, Wolfram's (1970) premise that "the purpose of teaching standard English is to assist students in adopting a dialect which is not socially stigmatized". The emphasis for creole situations is not so much on the replacement of "stigmatized" features, as on the acquisition of a secondary system in addition to native patterns of speech.

University of West Indies
St. Augustine, Trinidad

NOTES

1. For a study of the variable elements of Trinidadian English, and of the social context of that variation, see Winford, 1972.
2. According to the 1960 Census, the racial structure of the population of Trinidad and Tobago was as follows: of African descent, 43.3%; of East Indian descent, 36.5%; of mixed descent, 16.4%; Whites, 1.9%; Chinese, 1.0%; other, 1%; not stated .04%. (1960) Census, Vol. II, Part A, Table 5).
3. Both of the respondents citing this feature were Indians from rural areas.
4. All of these items were listed by the same informant.
5. Compare the discussion of social attitudes toward Creole in West Indian islands by W. A. Stewart (1962b).

REFERENCES

Alleyne, M. (1961), "Language and society in St. Lucia", *Caribbean Studies* I.
Baratz, Joan C. (1970), "Educational considerations for teaching Standard English to Negro Children", pp. 20–40 in: *Teaching Standard English in the Inner City*, ed. by R. Fasold and R. Shuy. Washington, D. C., Center for Applied Linguistics.
Berry, J. (1961), "English loanwords and adaptations in Sierra Leone Krio", pp. 3–16 in: *Creole Language Studies II: Proceedings of the Conference on Creole Language Studies*, ed. by R. Le Page. London, Macmillan.
Carrington, L. (1971), "Implications of the nature of the Creole continuum for sequencing educational materials". Mimeo. St. Augustine, University of the West Indies.
Cohen, R. A. (1969), "Conceptual styles, culture conflict and non-verbal tests of intelligence", *American Anthropologist* 71 (5):828–44.
Craig, D. (1971), "Education and Creole English in the West Indies", in: *Pidginization and Creolization of Languages*, ed. by D. Hymes. Cambridge University Press.
Herman, Simon R. (1961), "Explorations in the social psychology of language choice", *Human Relations* 14 (2):149–64.

Hunt, Chester L. (1966), "Language choice in a multilingual society", *Sociological Inquiry* 36 (2):240–53.

Hymes, D. (1968), "On communicative competence". Mimeo. Pennsylvania University.

Labov, W. (1964), "Stages in the acquisition of Standard English", pp. 77–104 in: *Social Dialects and Language Learning*, ed. by R. Shuy. Champaign, Illinois, National Council of Teachers of English.

Shuy, R. (1970), "Teacher training and urban language problems", pp. 120–41 in: *Teaching Standard English in the Inner City*, ed. by R. Fasold and R. Shuy. Washington, D.C., Center for Applied Linguistics.

Stewart, W. A. (1962), "Creole languages in the Caribbean", pp. 34–53 in: *Study of the Role of Second Languages in Africa, Asia and Latin America*, ed. by F. Rice. Washington, D.C., Center for Applied Linguisitcs.

Winford, D. (1972), "A Socio-linguistic description of two communities in Trinidad". Unpublished Ph.D. thesis, University of York.

Wolfram, W. A. (1970), "Sociolinguistic implications for educational sequencing", pp. 105–19 in: *Teaching Standard English in the Inner City*, ed. by R. Fasold and R. Shuy, Washington, D.C., Center for Applied Linguistics.

RAE A. MOSES, HARVEY A. DANIELS, AND ROBERT A.
GUNDLACH

Teachers' Language Attitudes and Bidialectalism

Over the past few years, linguists and educators have been engaged in a
noisy and sometimes angry debate over the problem of language
variation in American schools. The central focus of this dispute has been
on what, if anything, schools should do to change the language of black
American children. The controversy has been healthy in that it has
brought to public and professional attention some questions about
language which rarely receive much consideration: What are dialects?
How do some speech styles come to be favored over others? What is
appropriate language? What is the responsibility of schools in the
development of childrens' speech? While these issues are far from
settled, the typical response to them in American schools has been the
development of a wide range of language programs generally referred to
as bidialectal. Such programs have in common the goal of adding some
version of "Standard American English" to the child's speech repertoire
while upholding the usefulness and integrity of his natural dialect.

   In this paper, we hope to bring some new insight to the question of how
teachers' language attitudes affect the implementation of bidialectal
language programs. In this connection, we feel that one neglected and
potentially fruitful focus of study is the history and evolution of American
teachers' attitudes towards children's language. While the social and
politicial issues surrounding the dispute over Black English have a
distinctly modern flavor, some of the questions now being raised have
been familiar to the teaching profession for several decades. By examining these past controversies, we hope to provide a fuller context for
understanding the current dilemma. Towards this end, our paper first
presents a summary of the language difference issue during the last
decade, and then moves to review the history of teachers' language
attitudes over the last fifty years. Given this broader historical frame-

work, we should be better able to assess the feasibility and likelihood of
attitude change among American teachers in connection with contemporary bidialectal programs.

During the past twenty years, some important changes have taken
place in the sociolinguistic environment of the American public school
classroom. Partly as a result of the 1954 *Brown vs. the Board of Education
of Topeka* Supreme Court decision, whole "new" groups of students
began to enter integrated schools, and brought with them dialects and
speech styles not previously encountered by their teachers. In the first
ten years following the court's decision, not much attention was paid to
the expanding range of language found in the schools. In the early
1960's, however, active interest in this question was sparked. As part of
the sudden increase in the study of minority groups during this period,
the "substandard" language spoken by these children quickly became a
matter of professional concern.

The work which finally spurred some study of minority dialects in the
early sixties, oddly enough, involved not American blacks but lower-
class speakers of British English. Basil Bernstein, in a series of articles
beginning in 1958,[1] offered a social theory of speech based on a model of
elaborated and *restricted* codes. In this theory, the development of
particular speech systems is tied to the nature of social relations in the
environment in which they originate: thus, "the particular form of a
social relation acts selectively on what is said, when it is said, and how it is
said; the form of the social relation regulates the options that speakers
take up at both syntactic and lexical levels". Based on his examination
of middle-class homes, Bernstein concluded that children raised in this
environment "are oriented towards receiving and offering universalistic
meanings", while children from lower-class homes speak a language
which "creates social solidarity at the cost of the verbal elaboration of
individual experience" (Bernstein 1970: 28–29).

It was not surprising that Bernstein's speculations were immediately
and enthusiastically applied to the study of the language of American
minority children. Here, at a time when the problems of black children
were suddenly arousing new interest, was a conceptual framework into
which the divergences of "Black English" might be fitted and perhaps,
pedagogical applications derived therefrom. The theory did seem to
account for some observed facts: the apparent simplification of "Standard
English" which characterized the black dialect; the strong collective
sense among its speakers, as well as the academic failure of many of its

speakers. Unfortunately, Bernsteins' terminology of "restricted" and "elaborated" language was quickly translated as "inferior" and "superior" in the American context, in spite of the theorist's attempts to preclude such oversimplification.

The influence of Bernstein's work first surfaced in a United States Office of Education Conference on "Improving English Skills for Culturally Different Youth" held in 1962. The enthusiastic if simplistic embrace of Bernstein's model is found in the papers of several participants. Marjorie Smiley, in a review of recent research, offered the following:

Bernstein's analysis of lower-class speech in England leads him to conclude that such speech is not merely different but deficient. To describe it merely as a dialect, though it may be this as well, is to miss the fact that the simplifications in language structure characteristic of lower-class speech make it almost impossible to formulate intellectual generalizations (Jewett, Mersand, and Gunderson 1964: 58).

In view of the traditional American conception of black intellectual inferiority, this new deficit construct seemed to be a logical addition to the explanation of minority culture and behavior.

English teachers as a group were quick to hop on the deficit bandwagon, and a National Council of Teachers of English report in 1965:

The inability of the disadvantaged child to express himself is one of the first noticeable things about him. ... By the time that they are five years old, disadvantaged children of almost every kind are typically one to two years retarded in language development. This is supported by virtually any index of language development one cares to look at (NCTE 1965: 10–11).

By the middle sixties, a fairly firm and confident consensus had been forged among the psychologists and English teachers studying the question of language differences in the schools. These divergent speech styles were the product of deprived environments; they were "substandard" if not downright inferior; and they posed intellectual, educational, and occupational handicaps to their speakers.

It was into this forbidding environment that linguists first stepped with some contradictory, and often inflammatory evidence. No, said McDavid (1964), Labov (1967), Shuy (1969), and others, these social dialects are not linguistically inferior. Just the opposite, they argued, Black English is a fully developed, rule-governed, and natural language which simply cannot be written off as sloppy, inadequate, or inferior. The battle was joined, and over the next few years a tremendous amount of linguistic evidence began piling up in favor of this "new" view of social dialects. Stewart (1970), Dillard (1972), and others set off to describe the evolution of Black English, in an attempt to reinforce its legitimacy by presenting its historical origins. Kochman (1969) directed his attention to the study of unique, specialized black speech behaviors: sounding, rapping, playing the dozens, and the like. Labov (1972), in perhaps the single most important line of research, set out to prove that black children, when observed in a natural linguistic environment, will be found to have normally developed language. The contribution of these and other efforts has already been acknowledged by the fact that references to substandard or inferior social dialects have all but disappeared from educational literature. And, in a kind of symbolic concession statement from English teachers, the Conference College Composition and Communication recently passed a resolution stating:

We affirm the students' right to their own patterns and varieties of language – the dialects of their nurture or whatever dialects in which they find their own identity and style. Language scholars long ago denied that the myth of a standard American dialect has any validity. The claim that any one dialect is unacceptable amounts to an attempt of one social group to exert its dominance over another. Such a claim leads to false advice for speakers and writers, and immoral advice for humans (CCCC 1974: 2–3).

But there is a paradox in all of this. Since the beginning of the linguists' assault on the problem, teachers have been unwilling to follow the evidence to its logical conclusion. Despite the omnipresent pedagogical pledges of respect for divergent language, the fact remains that virtually all school English programs continue to be aimed at the alteration of the language of minority children. Typical school practices continue to emphasize either eradication of nonstandard speech, or some version of bidialectalism.

About the former of these two approaches – eradication – there now seems to be a rhetorical consensus. No major spokesman for teachers, psychologists, or linguists currently espouses eradication as a viable or appropriate school language policy. And while the techniques of eradication continue to be practiced in many American classrooms, the fact remains that they are engaged in without the philosophical or practical support of the organized teaching profession. The quick decline of eradication as the treatment of choice for language problems, however, has been matched by the equally rapid rise in enthusiasm for bidialectalism as an alternative approach.

The question has been asked by James Sledd (1969, 1972) whether eradication and bidialectalism are in fact two different policies. While

Sledd seems to think not, we find that bidialectalism differs from eradication at least because it places new and more complex demands on the classroom teacher. As Karen Hess has pointed out:

The sensitivities of minority groups demand a new and humane basis for the teacher's actions in teaching a standard English – namely, the understanding that a standard English is taught not because it is "correct", but because it is a socially, educationally, and vocationally useful dialect. This requirement suggests a reorientation of teachers from an absolutist to a relativistic attitude toward language – an orientation which may be contrary to the current value systems of many teachers (Hess 1973: 27).

As we can see, Hess' charge to teachers suggests some behaviors clearly different from those requisite to the cheerless, authoritarian task of eradication.

Exactly what have Hess and the bidialectalists asked English teachers to do differently? Teachers are urged, first of all, to give up their old notions of correctness and take on a more pragmatic view of their students' language – that is, *to change their professional attitudes towards language*; and they are exhorted to become more "humane", take on a more "relativistic" orientation, and to alter their "value systems" – that is, to *change their personal attitudes toward language*. While this dichotomous construct of personal and professional attitudes may not be technically accurate, we offer it in order to suggest that teachers of language possess not only their individual attitudes about language and its uses, but also have language attitudes arising out of the traditions, roles, and responsibilities of their jobs. Put another way, we might simply say that teachers are likely to have at least more complex, and perhaps more deeply-rooted language attitudes than has generally been recognized, and that when we demand their alteration we must do so with a better understanding of the task involved.

It has always been at least crudely recognized that teachers seem to have a large attitudinal investment in language standards. Writers on language have voiced a surprisingly uniform view of the English teacher in this connection:

... there is a tradition in America that the English teacher has an obligation to impose a rigid standard on his students, so that the revelation of one's professional identity in a social situation is likely to curdle the conversation with such remarks – not always in jest – that the others had better watch their grammar (McDavid 1969: 92).

For all the attention devoted by language scholars to the precise definition of the word *grammar*, misunderstanding and misapplication prevail.... The frequently heard remark "Watch your grammar, he's an English teacher!" relates to (this misunderstanding) (Jensen 1974: 101).

Indeed, the very knowledge that one is a teacher of English will, upon occasion, embarrass those with whom he engages in conversation. They will apologize for their own ineptitude in their native tongue and accordingly feel, or claim to feel, certain constraints upon their natural instincts toward self-expression. "So you're an English teacher. I'll have to watch my grammar" (Marckwardt 1966: 7).

Subservience to, or at least faith in, the traditional school discipline in English is a very notable and potent characteristic of American English. Teacher knows best in such matters as correct grammar, though she may be regarded as a complete booby and a crashing bore in all other departments (Pyles 1972: 163).

These comments tell us a good deal about the language attitudes of teachers, if we are willing to accept the reputational evidence. While these writers certainly do not endorse the public view, they suggest that people react to English teachers as absolutist defenders of the mother tongue.

The absolutist-relativist controversy, it seems, has been with us for quite some time. Wallace Douglas (1969) has pointed out that John Locke fought out this issue with himself in 1694, resolving it in favor of something resembling the current idea of bidialectalism. While Locke first asserts that languages "were made not by rules, or art, but by accident, and the common use of people", he goes on to examine the question, "Is grammar then of no use?". Almost none, Locke implies, though he allows that its study may be appropriate for gentlemen in high public office whose speech must avoid "shocking the ears of those it is adressed to which solecisms and offensive irregularities". As Douglas notes, Locke's idea that the effectiveness of a communication relies on its propriety has had an "enormous importance in the development of the English curriculum in this country" (Douglas 1969: 158ff.).

Douglas would seem to be right as we begin to consider the American version of the absolutist-relativist controversy. Shortly after American English teachers had established the National Council of Teachers of English, this issue quickly surfaced. In 1918, an NCTE affiliate began sponsoring Better Speech Week, and devised the following pledge for students:

I love the United States of America. I love my country's flag. I love my country's language. I promise:

1. That I will not dishonor my country's speech by leaving off the last syllable of words.
2. That I will say a good American "yes" and "no" in place of an Indian grunt "um-hum" and "nup-um" or a foriegn "ya" or "yeh" and "nope".
3. That I will do my best to improve American speech by avoiding loud rough tones, by enunciating distinctly, and by speaking pleasantly, clearly, and sincerely.
4. That I will learn to articulate correctly as many words as possible during the year[2] (Gawthorp 1965: 9–10).

In the same era, a number of voices were raised against the inanities of Better Speech Week and its absolutist mentality. In 1920, W. P. Reeves wrote in the *English Journal* that American dialects and idioms were not only natural and healthy, but also a positive expression of the diversity of American culture (Gawthorp 1965: 11–12). During the 1920's, there were increasing suggestions from NCTE members that instruction in traditional grammar should be discarded. In 1929, C. H. Matrauers suggested that language be taught not according to arbitrary rules, but according to the social and occupational needs of students. The relativist position gained strength, and by the end of the decade, the NCTE had been forced to withdraw its support of Better Speech Week (Gawthorp 1965: 10–14).

In an attempt to settle the absolutist-relativist controversy, the NCTE sponsored several monographs on usage, beginning in 1927. These studies, conducted first by Sterling Leonard (1932) and later by Marckwardt and Walcott (1938), all tended to show that English teachers were trying to preserve in the classrooms niceties of language long since abandoned even by the most educated speakers in the language community. By 1935, these findings had prompted an NCTE commission to declare:

Good English is that form of speech which is appropriate to the speaker, true to the language as it is, and comfortable to the speaker and listener. It is the product of custom, neither cramped by rule nor freed from all restraint; it is never fixed, but changes with the organic life of the language (Lightner 1965: 23).

In the same year, however, Albert Marckwardt took several pages of the *English Journal* to declare that the attitudes of English teachers seemed little affected by nearly a decade of persistent argument by the relativists of the era (Lightner 1965: 22). As if to confirm his concern, the late 1930's saw a rash of articles demanding that English teachers return to the basic, traditional grammar instruction which had previously been their main occupation.

In spite of the unwillingness of many English teachers to accept relativistic notions of language, the NCTE continued to support precisely this position. In a 1943 column on usage, the editors of *English Journal* instructed:

The forms of *don't* and *doesn't* in the third person singular are rival forms, differing in connotation. Both are very old, both widespread among native English speakers, both immediately intelligible, both "pure" English.... There is, however, in certain groups a prejudice against *don't*; the speaker will find this a handicap to him (exactly as he will find bad table manners a handicap) in these groups (Lightner 1965: 28–9).

This extremely clear statement of the NCTE position was followed, for the next ten years, by argument after argument in its support. But in spite of the quieting voices of opposition, the NCTE in 1952 found it necessary to point out that few changes had taken place in the classroom practices of English teachers:

No story is more exciting than the successful battle of the National Council of Teachers of English to liberalize the teaching of English usage.... But (the) facts, all available in print, many of them for a decade or more, are not generally known by teachers of English.... We have secured, at length, a partial acceptance of the truths about language which every linguist takes for granted. But the battle is not yet won (Meyers 1965: 46).

The editorial was charitable in its choice of words. It gently urged its constituency to get the facts, but it is also clear that the editorial writers were seeking a change in attitudes and practices as well. The editorial was also charitable, or perhaps mistaken, in failing to trace the controversy back to its roots in the 1920's, rather than simply in the preceding "decade or more".

The debate was focused but hardly resolved in subsequent years. In 1956, another NCTE commission presented a more schematic view of the relativist line:

(1) language changes constantly; (2) change is normal and represents not corruption but improvement; (3) spoken language is the language; (4) correctness rests on usage; (5) all usage is relative (Russell 1965: 49).

Objections continued to be raised, although some took a less antagonistic tone than had previously characterized absolutist rejoinders. In 1958, David Conlin reasoned that traditional grammar and usage instruction was not likely to be given up by teachers largely because such instruction was "such a massive element in our teaching culture" (Russell 1965: 53).

Conlin's statement aptly summarized forty years of controversy between absolutist and relativist teachers of English. While the relativist group was clearly in control of the organized profession during the entire period, its apparent impact on the attitudes and practices of teachers was small. The long-standing occupational and personal attitudes of teachers towards language blocked significant changes in classroom practice. From all we can tell, the preoccupation of English teachers with "correct" language abated only modestly during this period.

In the 1950's, as the debate over correctness and usage began to subside, a new and related issue came to the fore. Oscar Haugh offered one of the first explicit descriptions of this problem in 1955:

There are only two kinds of English, standard and substandard. It is substandard, of course, which we must try to eradicate from both the students' speaking and writing. On the other hand, there are two varieties of standard English, the formal and the informal. . . (Russell 1965: 51).

English educators, it seems, had finally discovered cultural diversity in the classroom.

Studying the writings of English teachers over the past fifteen years, we find that the debate over nonstandard English – the language of "culturally different" students – seems to have taken the place of the controversy over usage. It is important to note that the debates of the past had generally concerned practices in segregated white schools, and the subject of genuinely divergent dialects was rarely raised in this context. Even the most benign of the early relativists would probably have blanched at the thought that his cries for teacher acceptance of students' language might be extended to, for example, black dialect-speaking children. Equally important is the continuity and interrelation of these two issues. Whether teachers are dealing with usage issues in a homogenous population of white students, or with language practices in a culturally mixed classroom, the same teacher attitudes are brought into play. Though the presence of significantly divergent dialects may place a greater strain on the language attitudes of teachers, the fact remains that the same capacity for a relativistic outlook is being tested.

As we have already indicated, the teachers' debate over language policies for "culturally different" students began in full force during the early 1960's. Some of the propositions about divergent language advanced by educators and psychologists during this period clearly suggest attitudes descended more from the absolutist than the relativist heritage. A 1965 NCTE Task Force report asserts:

Furthermore they (black students) are not in the habit of expressing subjective emotions and feelings, a very important possibility of language. . . . (Another) major function of language in its role on the process of thought, is the assimilation of specific pieces of information into meaningful concepts. The disadvantaged child has an even less adequate grasp of this use of language than he has of language as a means of expression (NCTE 1965: 12, 14).

While this statement was consistent with the overall tenor of the period, it was hardly the most critical of black childrens' linguistic capabilities.

One of the most influential teams working and teaching in the area of language variation, Bereiter and Englemann, claimed in 1966 that disadvantaged black children essentially had no language at all, and that their vocal output consisted of primitive animal cries emitted as an accompaniment to action (Bereiter and Englemann 1966: 112–113).

The work of linguists began to show itself in the writings and policies of educators around 1967, as bidialectalism increasingly came to be espoused as the solution to the problem. Linguists had, of course, argued vigorously that the language of "disadvantaged" students was as linguistically sound, organized and powerful as any other tongue – and suggested, sometimes in emphatic terms, that teachers face and accept this fact before attempting to deal with their students' divergent language. That teachers would accept the relativistic rhetoric of bidialectalism without adopting its assumptions was probably to be expected in light of the evolution of teachers' language attitudes in general. But the extent of the breakdown in communication between linguists and educators was massive, and it deprived proposed bidialectal programs of accurate or appropriate implementation.

In a 1967 article on "English Programs for the Disadvantaged", Richard Corbin suggested that:

Education for the disadvantaged means chiefly English for the disadvantaged, since our language is central to all other aspects of culture.... Without some involvement in our literature, (the black student) has small chance of lighting the fires of his imagination or gauging and pushing out towards the horizons of his humanity (Corbin 1967: 79).

Corbin caps his discussion by offering sympathy to teachers who must toil in schools where "four letter words carry more weight than Elizabethan poetry", but exhorts them to assist black children in their escape from the "damp, cold, cockroach-and-rat infested, poemless slum" (Corbin 1967: 80, 82). More important than the racist tinge here is the way in which Corbin has mistranslated the assumptions underlying bidialectalism. Respect for, and acceptance of children's own language can hardly coexist with the messianic promotion of "our language" as the key to human growth.

Corbin was not alone during this period, and similar misapplications of bidialectal theory abound in the literature. Writing on "Ways to Improve Oral Communication of Culturally Different Youth", Ruth Golden offers this set-piece rationale for the questioning student:

We say to them "This brand of English you are using is a language in itself, which may have its uses for you. It is like an old suit of clothes which we do not want to throw away because we may still want to wear it on some occasions. But we would not think of wearing the old suit for a job interview or a dance, if we have something better to wear. Here in this class you can acquire the language used by most Americans in the business world. This language will then be yours to use when you want and need it" (Golden 1964: 104).

Quite unlike the bidialectalist approach which linguists had suggested, Golden's rationale assumes the superiority of standard English, the slight usefulness of the children's dialect, and even the patriotic virtue of talking right in the "business world".

Karen Hess' injunction that teachers must change their "value systems" and move from "an absolutist to a relativistic attitude toward language" brings us up to the present. While her confidence in the ability of teachers to adopt more realistic language attitudes may be admirable, the historical context which we have tried to provide offers little support for such optimism. American English teachers have been fighting the absolutist-relativist battle for at least fifty years without resolving it. And in spite of the generally progressive stance of the profession's leadership, it would seem that the "teaching culture", with its long-established blend of attitudes, beliefs, prejudices, and roles has prevented the adoption of a widespread and genuinely relativistic view of language among teachers.

With what tools have bidialectalists expected to work this change on the language attitudes of teachers? Again, Karen Hess offers a typical suggestion:

It is widely contended, though as yet unproven, that a relativistic attitude toward language will emerge if teachers and students acquire more knowledge about dialects, particularly nonstandard dialects, from a socio-historical perspective. However, it has repeatedly been observed that teachers are generally uninformed about dialects (Hess 1973: 27–8).

On the heels of this statement, Hess provides a number of specific suggestions about the various kinds of linguistic knowledge which, if in the possession of teachers, might successfully work the appropriate attitude change. These include "... general linguistic knowledge of language as well as specific knowledge of those dialects spoken by their students" (Hess 1973: 28).

While the theme of providing teachers with more information about language runs through the recommendations of many modern bidialectalists, at least four of the most prominent linguists working in this area are less than confident about this approach. In a recent article on language programs for preschool children, Cazden, Baratz, Labov, and Palmer (1973: 387) take up the question of teacher attitudes and the prospects for changing them. Reviewing recent research, they first affirm that teachers do indeed "evaluate children more negatively when their speech has nonstandard pronunciation and syntax". Their conclusion, however, contradicts the assertion that these attitudes will change appropriately in the presence of "the facts" about dialects:

We do not know how a training program for teachers should be designed to deal with such ethnocentric biases. Since these reactions are deeply founded in the teacher's own past experiences, they probably will not be changed merely by learning the facts of language differences (p. 388).

Such a statement, particularly as it comes from four of the most searching students of American social dialects, demands our consideration.

It is interesting to note that the caution expressed by Cazden, Baratz, Labov, and Palmer in 1973 has historical roots of its own. Earlier in this paper, we described a 1943 statement of the NCTE leadership in which they decried the failure of the "facts" about usage to work any significant change in the attitudes or practices of English teachers. Every available source of insight about teachers' language attitudes, it seems, suggests not optimism but caution about the prospects for changing them with a mere application of knowledge.

Those of us who have attempted to devise teacher-training programs aimed at changing attitudes have faced the complexity of this issue firsthand. Robbins Burling describes his difficulties in setting up such a program for Detroit teachers:

I have tried to organize a course that would focus upon the nature of nonstandard English and the implications of the dialect for education. I have tried to use this course to reach teachers, but I have had trouble persuading them that I had anything useful to say. . . . I have found that teachers and linguists start with such different assumptions and such a different outlook on language that they often find difficulty in talking to each other (Burling 1971: 222).

This is an experience we have shared as the three of us, in various combinations, have taught a similar course a half-dozen times at Northwestern University. Called "Cross-Cultural Communication in the Urban Classroom", our program was implicitly designed to alter the language attitudes of the preservice teachers enrolled. Like Burling, we have been forced by the results of early attempts to adjust our aims and techniques, and to reconsider our own expectation that our students' language attitudes would quickly undergo significant changes.

In our attempts to understand these difficulties, and gain guidance for more realistic approaches, we find some comfort in Fishman and Agheyisi's recent paper on language attitude studies. They emphasize this simple but crucial fact: "The concept 'attitude' has been variously defined and characterized by almost every theorist or researcher who has concerned himself with attitude studies" (Fishman and Agheyisi 1970: 137). We simply do not yet know what an attitude is, how it operates, or, certainly, how it changes. The only point on which students of language attitudes seem to agree, Fishman and Ageheyisi note, is that "attitudes are learned from previous experience, and that they are not momentary but relatively enduring" (p. 139). The rudimentary state of knowledge about the nature and operation of language attitudes, then, may help to explain why programs designed to change them have been generally unsuccessful.

Our review of the roles of teacher language attitudes in school programs has confirmed their significance. Nothing in our analysis has led us to suppose that the beliefs of teachers do not have enormous, probably critical, importance in the development of the sociolinguistic environment of the classroom, as well as in the success or failure of non-absolutist school language programs. We have found, most importantly, that new approaches to working with children's language – like bidialectalism – do in fact demand substantial changes in the language attitudes of teachers, and that such changes are extremely unlikely to occur in the near future.

All of this should not be construed to represent an altogether pessimistic outlook on our part. Obviously, an individual teacher's language attitudes can and do change as a result of experience, instruction, and other factors operating in an effective but as yet unknown way. We simply mean to indicate that any language program which contains as one of its prerequisites an alteration in the language attitudes of teachers must, if it is to be realistic, understand and take account of the massive and persistent factors which work against this goal.

Northwestern University

NOTES

1. For example, see Basil Bernstein, "Some Sociological Determinants of Perception", *British Journal of Sociology*, Vol. 9, 1958; and, "A Public Language: Some Sociological Implications of a Linguistic Form", *British Journal of Sociology*, Vol. 10, 1959; for a more recent version of the theory, see "A Sociolinguistic Approach to Socialization: With Some References to Educability", *Language and Poverty*, Frederick Williams (ed.) (Chicago, Markham, 1971), pp. 25–61.
2. Much of the historical material used in this section of the paper is drawn from "An Examination of the Attitudes of the NCTE Toward Language", Raven I. McDavid (ed.), National Council of Teachers of English Research Report No. 4, Champaign, Illinois, 1965.

REFERENCES

Bereiter, Carl, and Engelmann, Sigfried (1966), *Teaching Disadvantaged Children in the Preschool.* Englewood Cliffs, New Jersey, Prentice Hall.

Bernstein, Basil (1958), "Some Sociological Determinats of Perception", *British Journal of Sociology* 9:159–174.

— (1970), "A Sociolinguistic Approach to Socialization: With Some References to Educability", pp. 25–61 in: *Language and Poverty*, ed. by F. Williams. Chicago, Markham Publishing Company.

Burling, Robbins (1971), "Talking to Teachers about Social Dialects", *Language Learning* 21, (2):221–34.

Cazden, Courtney B., Baratz, Joan C., Labov, William, and Palmer, Francis H. (1973), "Language Development in Day Care Programs", pp. 377–96 in: *Revising Early Childhood Education* ed. by J. Frost. New York, Holt, Rinehart and Winston.

Conference of College Composition and Communication (1974), "Students' Rights to Their Own Language", *College Composition and Communication*, Special Issue.

Corbin, Richard (1967), "English Programs for the Disadvantaged", *NASSP Bulletin* 51:78–82.

Dillard, J. L. (1972), *Black English: Its History and Usage in the United States.* New York, Random House.

Douglas, Wallace (1969), "The History of Language Instruction in the Schools", pp. 155–66 in: *Linguistics in School Programs*, ed. by A. Marchuardt. Chicago, National Society for the Study of Education.

Fishman, Joshua, and Agheyisi, Rebecca (1970), "Language Attitude Studies: A Brief Survey of Methodological Approaches", *Anthropological Linguistics* 12 (5).

Gawthorp, Betty (1965), "1911–1929", pp. 7–16 in: *An Examination of the Attitudes of the NCTE Toward Language*, ed. by R. McDavid, National Council of Teachers of English Research Report No. 4. Champaign, Illinois, NCTE.

Golden, Ruth I. (1964), "Ways to Improve Oral Communication of Culturally Different Youth", pp. 100–9 in: *Improving English Skills of Culturally Different Youth*, ed. by Jewett, Mersand, and Gunderson. Washington, D.C., Office of Education.

Hess, Karen (1973), "Dialects and Dialect Learning: Where We're At", *English Education* 5 (1):26–34.

Jensen, Julie M. (1974), "On Linguistic Insecurity: A Report of Usage Fieldwork of Preservice Teachers", *English Education* 5 (2):101–5.

Jewett, Arno, Mersand, Joseph, and Gunderson Doris V., (eds.) (1964), *Improving English*

Skills of Culturally Different Youth. Washington, D.C., U.S. Office of Education, Department of Health, Education and Welfare.

Kochman, Thomas (1969), "Culture and Communication: Implications for Black English in the Classroom", *Florida Foreign Language Reporter*, Spring-Summer 1969.

Labov, William (1967), "Some Sources of Reading Problems for Negro Speakers of Nonstandard English", pp. 140–67 in: *Directions in Elementary English*, ed. by A. Frazier. Champaign, Illinois, NCTE.

— (1972), *Language in the Inner City*. Philadelphia, University of Pennsylvania Press.

Leonard, Sterling A. (1932), *Current English Usage*, English Monograph No. 1. Champaign, Illinois, NCTE.

Lightner, C. Michael (1965), "1930–1945", pp. 17–30 in: *An Examination of Language Attitudes of the NCTE Toward Language*, ed. by R. McDavid. National Council of Teachers of English Research Report No. 4. Champaign, Illinois, NCTE.

McDavid, Raven I. (1964), "Dialectology and the Teaching of Reading", *The Reading Teacher* 18 (3):206–13.

— (1965), *An Examination of the Attitudes of the NCTE Toward Language*, National Council of Teachers of English Research Report No. 4. Champaign, Illinois, NCTE.

— (1969), "The Concept of a Linguistic Standard", pp. 85–108 in: *Linguistics in School Programs*, ed. by A. H. Marckwardt. Chicago, National Society for the Study of Education.

Marckwardt, Albert H., and Walcott, Fred (1938), *Facts About Current English Usage*, English Monograph, No. 3. Champaign, Illinois, NCTE.

— (1966), *Linguistics and the Teaching of English*, Bloomington, Indiana, Indiana Press.

— (1969), *Linguistics in School Programs*. Chicago, National Society for the Study of Education.

Meyers, Doris C. (1965), "1945–1954", pp. 31–46 in: *An Examination of the Attitudes of NCTE Toward Language* ed. by R. McDavid. National Council of Teachers of English Research Report No. 4. Champaign, Illinois, NCTE.

National Council of Teachers of English (1965), *Language Programs for the Disadvantaged*. Champaign, Illinois, NCTE.

Pyles, Thomas (1972), "English Usage: The Views of the Literati", pp. 160–69 in: *Contemporary English: Change and Variation*, ed. by D. L. Shores. New York, J. B. Lippincott.

Shuy, Roger W. (1969), "A Linguistic Background for Black Children", pp. 117–37 in: *Teaching Black Children to Read*, ed. by J. C. Baratz and R. W. Shuy. Washington, D.C., Center for Applied Linguistics.

Russell, Geraldine (1965), "1955–1973", pp. 47–62 in: *An Examination of the Attitudes of the NCTE Toward Language*, ed. by R. McDavid. National Council of Teachers of English Report No. 4. Champaign, Illinois, NCTE.

Sledd, James (1969), "The Linguistics of White Supremacy", *English Journal* 58 (9):1307–15.

— (1972), "Doublespeak Dialectology in the Service of Big Brother", *College English* 33 (4):439–56.

Stewart, William (1970), "Toward a History of American Negro Dialect", pp. 351–79 in: *Language and Poverty*, ed. by F. Williams. Chicago, Markham Publishing Company.

DENNIS R. CRAIG

Bidialectal Education: Creole and Standard in the West Indies

1. THE DEFINITION AND LOCATION OF BIDIALECTAL SITUATIONS

A bidialectal educational situation can be considered to exist where the
natural language of children differs from the standard language aimed at
by schools, but is at the same time sufficiently related to this standard
language for there to be some amount of overlap at the level of vocabulary
and grammar. Obviously, the amount of such overlap can be expected
to vary with different situations. In some cases, the two forms of speech
might possess sufficient common characteristics in phonology, lexis, and
syntax for them to be mutually intelligible; at the other extreme, the
relatedness of the two might be insufficient to produce mutual intel-
ligibility in continuous speech, though some commonality of lexis might
still be evident to speakers. In the latter case, a bidialectal situation would
approach very closely to a genuinely "bilingual" one.

Many of the West Indian countries where creole languages are spoken
do not possess educational situations that may be regarded as bidialectal
in the sense just stated since, in some of these countries, the Creole language bears no relationship to the standard language used or aimed at in
schools. The latter is the case, for example in different places within the
officially Dutch West Indian territories where Papiamentu (which is
Spanish/Portuguese-based), Sranan (which is English-based) or Sara-
maccan (which is also English-based) are some of the Creole languages.
In the latter territories, the educational situation, in the context of
Creole language has to be regarded as clearly bilingual.

Somewhat different from, though still relatively close to situations
like the latter are those existing in West Indian countries such as Haiti
and Martinique. In those countries, the base of the Creole is the same
language that is accepted as the official standard and language of edu-

cation: French. At the lexical level therefore there is a considerable relationship between Creole and Standard. Despite this, however, the phonological, morphological, and syntactic differences between the two forms of speech are wide enough to render them mutually unintelligible. There is some evidence, as discussed in Valdman (1969) for example, that in urban areas particularly, the occurrence of diglossia and the development of forms of speech intermediate between Creole and Standard might in time produce a situation equivalent to a bidialectal one; but at the present time, in the absence of large proportions of speakers whose habitual speech bridges the structural gap between Creole and Standard, the officially French-speaking West Indian countries, have to be regarded, like the Dutch countries, as giving rise to educational situations that are more bilingual than bidialectal.

In the officially English-speaking territories of the West Indies, however, where English-based Creoles either existed at some time in the past or still exist, processes of diglossia and the development of intermediate language varieties between Creole and Standard have proceeded much further than they have in the case of Haiti and Martinique just mentioned. In some of these officially English-speaking territories, as in the case of Trinidad and St. Vincent, for example, the original and extreme form of an English-based Creole has all but disappeared, and what remains are systems of linguistic items intermediate between Creole and Standard. DeCamp (1971) referred to such systems as the post-Creole speech continuum. The presence of this continuum led Stewart (1962) to suggest that the Creoles of Jamaica, Guyana, Belize and the non-standard speech of the other officially English-speaking West Indian territories may best be treated as regional varieties or dialects of English.

It can thus be seen that there is some justification for regarding the officially English-speaking West Indian countries as giving rise to bidialectal educational situations in a way in which the other countries do not; but it has to be noted that this difference between the officially English-speaking countries and countries like Haiti, for example, is one of degree rather than of kind. What has happened is that sociolinguistic history has caused countries like Jamaica and Guyana (both officially English-speaking) to have larger proportions of their populations speaking a language intermediate between Creole and Standard than Haiti has; but both of the former countries, however, still have considerable proportions of speakers whose habitual English-based Creole is just as incomprehensible to English ears as Haiti's French-based

Creole is to French ears; and most of the remaining officially English-speaking countries, although they have no discrete Creoles like those of Jamaica or Guyana, possess just as complex a range of continuum variation.

The officially English-speaking countries that give rise to bidialectal educational situations involving Creole and Standard language in the way so far explained have a total population of about five million speakers and are as follows: the Caribbean mainland territories of Guyana and Belize, together with the islands of Jamaica, Trinidad and Tobago, Grenada, Barbados, St. Vincent, St. Lucia, Dominica, Montserrat, St. Kitts, Nevis, Anguilla, Antigua, The Virgin Islands, The Cayman Islands, The Turks and Caicos Islands, and the Bahamas. Some of the mentioned islands, notably St. Lucia, Dominica, and Grenada have significant proportions of their populations who speak a French Creole exclusively or both a French and an English Creole.

In these countries, the monolingual speakers of Creole or Creole-influenced language, as will be further discussed subsequently, can be estimated to form about 70% to 80% of the total speakers. These Creole or Creole-influenced monolinguals would have a language that ranges from a basilect Creole to a mesolectal language intermediate between Creole and English. A social-class classification would put most of them within the levels of lower-working, working and lower-middle class. The language-education problem that they pose is experienced mainly in the public system of primary, all-age, and post-primary schools for which the governments of the respective countries are responsible.

2. THE NEGLECT AND REDISCOVERY OF CREOLE

One characteristic of educational policy in the countries mentioned is that, traditionally, Creole or Creole-influenced language has been treated in schools as if it did not exist, or as if it should be eradicated if it existed. One reason for the development of this attitude to Creole is to be found in the relationship, already mentioned, between Creole and Standard at the lexical level; because of this relationship, it was easy for educational planners in the past to feel that Creole was merely a debased form of the standard language, and that this debasement could be corrected merely by a sustained exercise of carefulness on the part of the learner. The fact that this attitude is caused by the apparent lexical relationship between Creole and Standard seems proved by the more favourable attitude towards Creole found in territories where there is no relationship between Creole and Standard. The favourable attitude towards Creole in the officially Dutch-speaking territories, is attested to for example in Stewart (1962: 53), as compared with both the officially French and English-speaking territories where the attitude tends to be the opposite.

Another reason for the traditional educational attitude of neglecting Creole or Creole-influenced language or attempting to eradicate it is to be found in historical factors. Stewart (1967) comments on some of these historical factors and shows that, by the seventeenth century, all the present-day distinctive features of Creole and Creole-influenced English had already developed in the Western hemisphere and that in the officially English-speaking territories especially, it was easy for the whites to consider Creole English to be "broken" or "corrupt" English and evidence of the supposed mental limitations of the black slave population. The historian Edward Long, for example, writing of Jamaica in 1774 pointed out that "the language of the Creoles is bad English larded with the Guinea dialect", and this was obviously the pervading opinion, relevant to all the West Indian territories, which was handed down over the next two centuries. After the abolition of slavery in the 1830's the British Government made some attempt over the next century to develop public systems of education within the territories of the region, and early educational reports on the West Indies, like the 1938 Latrobe Reports for example, occasionally mention the role of English as a unifying force between the diverse language groups: aboriginals and Africans, French, Spanish, and Dutch speakers; and after the middle of the century Chinese, Indians, and other speakers who had come into the region. But Creole or Creole-influenced language as such was never regarded as one of the foreign languages to be reckoned with, except that in territories like St. Lucia and Dominica, where speakers of French Creole were to be found, the reports of the educational officials sometimes showed concern over the French Creole problem.

It was not until the 1940's at the earliest that the problem of English in what was essentially a bidialectal educational situation (although at that time it still was not recognized as such) began to receive some attention. An example of such attention, which comes from Jamaica, but which is relevant to all the similar West Indian territories is to be seen in the report of the educational commission under L. L. Kandel (1946) which endorsed the viewpoint expressed by the Norwood Committee (1943) in Britain that there was need for alarm over the deficiencies of school-leavers' English. The Kandel report then pointed out that the need for alarm was even greater in Jamaica as there was a much more serious problem than that being experienced in Britain. Even at this relatively late period, however, the dominant attitude of schools towards Creole or Creole-influenced language continued to tend either towards ignoring it or towards eradicating it by forbidding children to speak it within the hearing of teachers; the child was invariably made to understand that his speech in school had to be "good" English.

This continued denial in the first half of the present century of the linguistic existence of the majority of West Indian speakers in the officially English-speaking territories occurred despite the fact that by the end of the 1920's, apart from general works on Creole like those of Van Name (1870), Schuchardt (1882–91), and the bibliography of Gaidoz (1881), there had been several studies and language collections, some going back to the previous century, and referring specifically to the officially English-speaking territories. These works are exampled in the writings of Russell (1868) relative to Jamaica; Bonkhurst (1888), Cruickshank (1916), Scoles (1885), and Van Sertima (1897, 1905) relative to Guyana; Cruickshank (1911) relative to Barbados, and Innis (1910, 1933) and Thomas (1869) relative to Trinidad. Conditions in the remaining territories would have been closely similar to those represented in these works.

In the relevant countries, however, independent of and despite the educational system, there were factors at work that at the present time can be seen as contributing to a gradually more favourable attitude towards Creole and Creole-influenced speech. Such speech had long become codified in folk tales and vernacular humor, song and drama. In many territories, the daily and weekly newspapers (the only frequent reading for a majority of the literate population) had found it attractive, for many years, to present, written "in the dialect" (i.e., in Creole or near-Creole language) regular humorous and satirical commentaries on daily local life. Within contemporary memory some examples of the latter, under their newspaper column-titles or writers' pseudonyms are Quow, Uncle Stapie (Guyana), Macaw, Boysie (Trinidad), Quashie (Jamaica), Lizzie and Joe (Barbados, Montserrat), Annie and Josephine (Grenada), and Chatty and Papsy (Nevis). This popular interest in the vernacular culminated in the late 1940's, at the same time as the first expressions of educational alarm (referred to above) over English language proficiency, in a growing number of Creole languages collections and commentaries like, for example, some of Louise Bennett's publications in Jamaica (e.g., Bennett, 1942, 1943, 1950), Frank Collymore's serialisations of "Words and phrases of Barbadian dialect" (e.g., Collymore 1952), and in Guyana a series of articles on aspects of Creole language by D. A. Westmaas and Richard Allsopp, respectively, in the journal *Kyk-Over-All* between 1948 and 1953.

This growth of popular literary interest in Creole might have had, by itself, some influence on attitudes in education, but in any case it was followed closely by another, probably inevitable development which is the one that really made some educational change imperative. This development referred to is the beginning of modern grammatical studies of Creoles in the officially English-speaking territories.

Some of the first results of such studies are to be seen in Taylor (1945, 1952, 1955, 1961, 1963, 1968), LePage (1952, 1955, 1957; ed., 1959), Bailey (1953, 1962, 1966), Allsopp (1958a and b, 1962), LePage and DeCamp (1960), Cassidy (1961), Alleyne (1961, 1963), and Cassidy and LePage (1967). This body of work includes descriptions of the phonology, lexis and grammar of Dominican and Jamaican Creoles, some aspects of the morphology and syntax of Guyanese Creole, consideration of some sociolinguistic factors in relation to St. Lucia and Jamaica, some early thoughts on how language studies in the West Indies might be further promoted, and some general descriptive comments on Caribbean Creoles not yet substantially dealt with. In this work, Jamaican Creole gets the most comprehensive treatment in terms of its syntax, lexicology, and segmental phonology. Obviously, most of the relevant West Indian territories that have been earlier listed here, received no attention in these studies and, apart from the work on Jamaica, no one country received any wide-ranging study. Nevertheless, the work cited here was very significant for the West Indian region as a whole because firstly it created a scientific framework within which interested persons involved with language in the region could observe linguistic facts in the territories to which the work referred; secondly, it permitted such persons to make comparisons, within this scientific framework, between linguistic facts as described in this work and facts as known, merely through informal experience, relevant to territories not yet formally studied. As a result of this work, and the possibility just mentioned to which it gave rise, it became possible for educators within the region to view West Indian language-education problems in a manner comparable to how problems of bilingualism or multilingualism might be viewed in contemporary times; although the existence of this possibility does not necessarily imply its actual realization or achievement.

Work such as the preceding has continued up to the present, with some of the more recent additions to it taking on increasingly theoretical forms: Bailey (1971), for example, suggested that distinctions might be drawn between basilectal and mesolectal forms of Creole by measuring the quantity and complexity of the transformational rules that separated the respective forms from both Standard English and basilect Creole; and DeCamp (1971) showed that linguistic forms in the continuum between Creole and Standard were not just an ordered collection among which speakers shifted in response to social situations, but that the forms of the continuum were implicationally linked, so that the presence of specific forms rendered certain others obligatory. Subsequently, following the work of Labov (e.g., 1971) and C. J. Bailey (e.g., 1969, 1970) in Hawaii, Bickerton (1971, 1971a, 1972, 1972a, 1973) pursued further implications of DeCamp's thesis and suggested that in the West Indian Creole continuum, as presumably also universally in all speech communities, variation within and between idioletcs existed as sets of implicationally linked characteristics that could not be described by static grammatical models. The developments apparent in these studies, contribute to grammatical theory generally as well as to knowledge of Creole language situations of the bidialectal or multidialectal type; the implications of these developments for bidialectal education will be considered subsequently.

Concurrently with these developments, and additional to work appearing in Hymes (ed., 1971), there have been several studies within the West Indies, some of them unpublished, that describe specific aspects of English-based Creole or mesolectal language and thereby contribute further to the kind of information that the educator needs for work in relevant situations; among the latter studies are the following: Carrington (1967, 1969), Allsopp (1965), Reisman (1961, 1965), Hughes (1966), Lawton, D. L. (1963, 1964, 1971), Solomon (1966), Christie (1969), Warner (1967), and Winford (1972); in addition, a collection of papers currently in preparation for publication (Craig, ed., forthcoming) includes some relevant additional writing of Berry, Cassidy, Spears, Edwards, Allsopp, and Solomon (see references) that is of a descriptive or theoretical linguistic kind, as well as some other work of educational relevance that will be mentioned subsequently. The descriptive and theoretical writings just cited add the following information to that provided by the earliest set of Creole language studies already mentioned: additional information on the lexis and phonology of Jamaican, Cayman, Barbadian, and Guyanese creoles (Cassidy, Lawton, Berry, Allsopp, Spears); information on the distribution and structure of French

creole in St. Lucia and Dominica (Carrington, Christie); tentative and
very general statements on the linguistic and sociolinguistic situation in
Belize (Allsopp 1965), Antigua (Reisman), and Grenada (Hughes);
information on the syntactic structure of Creole and post-Creole
language and the socio-linguistic situation in Trinidad (Warner,
Winford, Solomon), and Guyana (Edwards). This work is not even in
quality, and there is no comprehensive survey of the region as a whole,
but it is sufficient to show the distribution of Creole and mesolectal
language, the general nature of the language system in most territories,
and some more detailed treatment of one or two situations sufficient
to permit a degree of extrapolation to other situations where adequate
work has not yet been done.

3. THE USE OF THE VERNACULAR IN EDUCATION

Growth of knowledge about Creole language situations, such as that
outlined above for the West Indian Creole-English situation, coincided
with the growth of new nations in the Third World and an international
recognition of the need for these new nations to have educational systems that would be fully relevant in each case to the specific national
identity, environment, and goals; part of this recognition implied the
need for each child to receive at least his earliest education in the language
that was most natural to him: his mother tongue. In the light of this
recognition, the fiction, maintained for over a century, that Standard
English was the mother tongue of West Indian Creole-speaking or
Creole-influenced children could no longer be maintained. One of the
first concrete reactions to this recognition was the proposal that the
Creole or mesolectal language of children, in officially English-speaking
West Indian territories should be used as the language of primary, even
if for no other, education. An early example of such a suggestion is to be
seen in the UNESCO (1953) monograph on the use of vernacular
languages in education, where it was suggested that some of the officially
English-speaking territories in the West Indies were among the areas of
the world where creole languages might well be used in Education. Up
to the present, however, more than two decades after this suggestion,
none of these territories has attempted to implement it.

The chief reason why the Creole or Creole-influenced language of
West Indian children has not been used in education lies in deep-seated
community attitudes to Creole. The old official attitude of ignoring its

existence or advocating its eradication has already been mentioned. In the community at large, Creole language has generally been identified historically with slavery, and in more recent times with very low social status and lack of education. This feeling about creole exists even in the minds of its speakers, most of whom would attempt, if they can, to modify their speech in direction of Standard English in the presence of an English speaker, and would feel insulted if a stranger who is obviously non-Creole-speaking attempts to converse with them in Creole. In this context, even the most Creole-speaking of parents tend to regard Standard English as the language of social mobility, and would tend to think that anyone who suggests the use of Creole or Creole-influenced language in education is advocating the socio-economic repression of the masses. This attitude of Creole and Creole-influenced speakers towards English has been mentioned in Bailey (1964) with reference to Jamaica, but it is an attitude that is to be found in all the officially English-speaking West Indian countries. It is not any way unique to these countries however, as it is very similar to that attitude of non-Standard speakers in the U.S.A. which Wolfram (1970: 29) describes, and which has been responsible for the non-acceptance of dialect readers in some "black" English communities. Obviously, it is an attitude that can be expected in any situation which is essentially bidialectal in its nature, although there are some genuinely bilingual situations, like the Spanish/English situation in Puerto Rico and the Indian-languages/Spanish situation in Central America, where similar attitudes seem to be present.

In effect it is an attitude that represents a type of socio-psychological dualism in which the low-status language is stubbornly preserved by its speakers as a part of their identity and cultural integrity,but at the same time these very speakers resist any measures which, by extending the societal role of their own low-status language, might impede their children's acquisition of the accepted high-status language. At the base of the attitude is probably the very pragmatic realization that it is unlikely that the high-status language could ever be completely replaced, and that even if it is, its status in the wider world would still make it a very desirable acquisition.

Another very important reason why Creole or Creole-influenced language has not been used in education within officially English-speaking West Indian territories is to be found in the technical difficulties that would be involved. One such difficulty would be that of the standardization of the phonology and grammar of the non-Standard language and the choice of an orthography for it. It is possible, in the matter of phonology and orthography, that if the language of a territory is of a mesolectal kind without the existence of a basilect Creole, then solutions to the problem might be similar to those suggested in Stewart (1969) and Fasold (1969) for American black dialects where conventional English orthography is retained. In the latter cases, English orthography represents the underlying realities of the non-Standard "dialects" to such an extent that it is easily possible to use the same orthography and incidentally benefit from having a single writing system for all speakers. However, in cases like those of Jamaica and Guyana, where there are basilect Creoles departing farther from English than mesolectal language does, the use of an English orthography might be somewhat more problematical, especially when relationships between phonology and grammar are taken into consideration, although it would be possible for teachers to use English spellings and permit a wide range of variant speech renditions as has been suggested in DeCamp (1972). In the matter of standardizing Creole or Creole-influenced grammar, there are still larger problems, however, occasioned by the range of continuum variation to which persons have become accustomed, and the difficulty of deciding on the point of the continuum at which the standard grammar will be selected. The selection of basilect Creole would exclude most mesolectal speakers, and the selection of a mesolect would not solve the most serious societal problems of Creole speakers; an idea of the extent of the problem can easily be gauged by an examination of the wide variation that is possible in the Creole and Creole-influenced versions of Standard English sentences discussed in Craig (1971a: 374).

Assuming, however, that the linguistic, technical problems just mentioned can be overcome, there are problems of implementation and costs of action programmes of the kind discussed in Bull (1955), that would by themselves tend to induce governments to avoid the use of Creole or Creole-influenced language in education. First of all, in the West Indian territories relevant here, it would be necessary for a relatively large percentage (probably about 50%) of the professional people working in education to be taught the vernacular that is to be used. Textbooks and other educational materials would then need to be prepared in the vernacular in a situation where persons with the requisite skills would even in normal circumstances be very scarce. Even if, the use of the vernacular is confined to primary education, with the prestige language being introduced subsequently as a second language and used later as the language of instruction in secondary school, the financial cost, to a newly developing territory, of the measures just mentioned would be enormous and, except in the absence of a viable and nationally respectable alternative, quite likely prohibitive. Apart from all this, a country with the bidialectal type of Creole-language situation that is relevant here would need to consider seriously whether the use of the low-prestige language in the public system of schools and at a low level of education might not accentuate social divisions within the society rather than remove them, especially in a context where most children already attend primary schools and acquire some amount at least of mesolectal language, and where there is a selective system of secondary schools geared to the production of an educated elite. It is obvious that these considerations would not apply with equal force in all territories with bidialectal situations, and might not apply at all even in those Creole-speaking countries which approach the bidialectal type very closely (like Haiti, for example, where the relatively small proportion of children completing primary education and the 90% use of Creole within the society render such considerations inoperative). In the officially English-speaking West Indian territories, however, these considerations do apply and, together with what has already been said above about community attitudes, explain why governments have never seriously considered using the vernacular in education.

4. TEACHING THE STANDARD BY CORRECTION

When the educational use of Creole or Creole-influenced language is ruled out in a bidialectal situation such as the West Indian one, the most obvious alternative is for schools to employ a teaching strategy based on getting children to correct those characteristics of their own speech that differ from the language aimed at by schools. These are the characteristics which, in traditional school terminology would be regarded as resulting in language "errors" or "mistakes", and which the applied linguist would regard as contrasts between the native and target languages. The problem with this strategy of correction is that it leaves the learners completely at the mercy of the ad hoc and occasional intervention of the teacher, puts them in the position where they can learn only after they have made what they often come to regard as embarassing mistakes, and invariably makes them so aware of the possibility of mistakes that they become afraid and often incapable of expressing themselves in formal situations. In the older examples of the application of this strategy, some teaching of traditional English grammar would have formed a part of the classroom procedures, and in some ways this grammatical teaching was not altogether worthless, when carried out by intelligent teachers, as it gave the non-Standard speakers some logical framework within which they could systematize the "corrections" that they learned, and within which they could see the Standard language as a whole; there is no denying, however, that in many, probably a majority of cases, learners acquired merely a rote knowledge of one or two inaccurate grammatical rules which in no way affected their ability to express themselves in formal situations.

With the gradual popularization of modern linguistics and the demonstration by teachers and scholars like C. C. Fries (e.g., 1940, 1952) that traditional grammatical rules often misrepresented English as it is actually spoken, and also with a better understanding, through child-development studies (see, e.g., Carroll, 1969), of how language is learned, the teaching of "grammar" has declined in schools. However, present day survivals of the strategy of language-teaching by correction, with or without traditional grammar, can still be found in bidialectal classroom situations in the West Indies as well as elsewhere; in the U.S.A., for example, not so long ago, Crow *et al.* (1966: 124) showed the survival of this strategy when they stated:

Some of the causes of speech problems of the socially disadvantaged children are similar to those of listening. For example, a deficiency in auditory discrimination may result from the failure of parents to correct mistakes in spoken language, owing either to lack of knowledge of correct speech or to sheer indifference. Faulty auditory discrimination can be illustrated by the child's confusing the "th" sound with the "f" sound in a word such as "Mother" for which he may say "Muffer".

Correct speech is learned through imitation in the home and elsewhere. Many parents of socially disadvantaged children do not realize that their speech is incorrect and that their children's poor speech patterns are formed in the home. In school, corrective help is given, but the time is too short for much progress, and when the child returns home, he is confronted again with the inferior speech.

Like all advocates of a teaching-by-correction strategy, the writers of this extract make no use of the concept that low-social-status speech is, for all practical purposes, a dialect with its own distinctive rules of phonology and grammar and that the problem of learning standard speech is that of learning a new dialect. However, the importance of the home environment is well recognized, and it is precisely because of this environment that the strategy of teaching by correction inevitably fails, since that strategy has within it no way of systematically teaching sets of new language structure in such a way that they have a reasonable chance of persisting parallel to the language of the home.

In the West Indies, first in Jamaica and from there to other territories, a movement away from the correction strategy began in the late 1950's. It is well illustrated in this extract from Walters (1958), which it will be noted appeared fully eight years before Crow (*et al.*) already cited.

The general attitude to this problem has been that Jamaican Creole structure is wrong and must be corrected. Training College syllabuses in English have begun the first and second year courses with "Correction of common errors in speech", and "A more formal application of the rules of grammar to common errors in English in Jamaica", while the Code For Elementary Schools does say: "Spontaneity should not be discouraged by correction in the early stages" (Code of Regulations of the Education Department, 1938). A Training College principal recently announced, in a public discussion – "There is only one answer to the question of dialect – that is, it has no place whatever in our elementary schools", and a similar statement was circulated, in another territory, by the Inspector of Schools to all teachers. This attitude, that local speech is wrong and must not be allowed, held so firmly by educators and implemented in schools, has certainly had little effect on local speech, save to inhibit the spontaneous speech and writing in schools and produce a stilted and artificial style in the "educated".

A gradual change of attitude is being noted, however, as above when teachers are warned not to begin corrections too early and stifle spontaneity. A further step takes us away from the concept of "correcting wrong speech', towards learning a new way of saying things. A recently distributed directive on "The Curriculum Of Primary And Post Primary Schools" states: "The Jamaican vernacular is not the great obstacle to learning English it is generally supposed to be. It is a bridge to be used by the teacher to get to the use of the English language. There might well be the tacit understanding in our schools that English is the language spoken and written, but the Jamaican vernacular is understood". A revised syllabus for Jamaican Primary Schools suggests – "Interest must be aroused in speaking correct English as soon as possible, not as a matter of correcting what is wrong, but as acquiring new skill."

Enlightened as this change obviously was on the question of the "correction" strategy, it did not however, and probably could not at that point in time, have within it an understanding of all the linguistic realities that would have made a systematic approach to the language and reading problem fully possible. The approach then advocated was an "experience" approach which would get children to hear "new ways of saying things", induce them to say things in these new ways, and get them to read and write the new language. What was lacking in this approach was an orderly structure for the children's acquisition and production of the new language; by it, children came into contact with the new language fortuitously and at odd moments, just as they would in a completely first-language, or mother-tongue, educational situation, and there were no procedures within the advocated approach whereby the patterns and structures of the new language could be learned in such a way as not to be suppressed by the dominant home-language environment.

5. TEACHING THE STANDARD LANGUAGE AS A SECOND DIALECT

As has been pointed out already, the growth of Creole language studies in the West Indies after 1950 brought forcibly to people's attention the fact that Standard English, if not actually a foreign language, was clearly in the nature of a second dialect to most West Indians. One result of this awareness can be seen in the appearance in the West Indies of a number of writings which looked in various ways at the language-education problem and made suggestions about alleviating it. Including Walters (1958) already cited, the earliest of these language-educational studies were concerned with documenting what happened when Creole-influenced individuals at different levels of education attempted to receive and produce English, both in speech and writing. A statement of some of these is to be found in the Faculty of Education (1965) Report of the conference on linguistics, language teaching and the teaching of English, convened at the University of the West Indies. Some of these studies, like those of Craig (1964) and Grant (1964), were not system descriptive in a linguistic sense, but were concerned with error analyses, occurrence frequencies of various types of linguistic items and the comparisons that could be made, in these terms, between different social-class types and age-groups of learners. Studies of this kind seem useful for the planning of language-education in the region for several reasons. Firstly, in the context of the Creole/Standard continuum, actual frequency distributions of specific linguistic items give a more practical picture of the competence of speakers than static system-description can alone and by itself; secondly, there is the pragmatic educational necessity for teachers to be able to compare different types of learners and to perceive quantitative as well as qualitative language differences where these occur; and thirdly, in the absence of language development and performance data relevant to the West Indies, of the kind that can be found relevant to other societies, well evaluated and summarized in sources like Carroll (1960) and Denis Lawton (1968), for example, studies of this kind seem well justified in the circumstances of the West Indies.

Additional to the preceding, there began to appear at this time (in the early 1960's) several analyses of the classroom implications of Creole language-studies, indications of the quasi-foreign language nature of the language situation, and general suggestions for necessary teaching programmes in West Indian schools. Similar work has continued to appear up to the present and the relevant publications are Figueroa (1962, 1972), Gray (1963), Bailey (1963), Cuffie (1964), Jones (1966), and Carrington (1968, 1970). Some very recent additions to work of this kind are to be seen in Carrington (1971), Allsopp (1972), Edwards (1972), and Solomon (1972) where the language-teaching implications of specific phonological, lexical and syntactic characteristics of West Indian Creole or continuum language are examined. This most recent work differs from what preceded it by having its language-teaching considerations limited in each case to some single, specific aspect of linguistic form: implicational relationships in the continuum, prosodic features, morpho-syntactic variation in items like "have" and "be", and so on. It supplements the thesis of the foreign-language or quasi-foreign language nature of the language situation by a relatively in-depth analysis of the related linguistic form in each case, and what it would mean to teach an area of the Standard language that corresponds to or is related to that aspect of linguistic form. The problems of the total content of the language programme for children, its classroom implementation, and wider educational issues such as valid goals and the strategies for achieving these are not objects of immediate concern in this work.

By the middle of the 1960's, the resemblance between the Creole language situations in the officially English-speaking West Indies and the non-Standard English problems in the United States of America had been perceived. Stewart, who in 1964 had participated in the West Indian conference responsible for the Faculty of Education (1965) Report already cited, edited in the same year the influential "Non-Standard Speech and the Teaching of English". In the latter, the Jamaican language situation received a significant treatment, and the point is strongly made that foreign language teaching methods seem necessary in the quasi-foreign language situations of Creole and other non-Standard speakers in officially English-speaking countries, including the United States of America. Appearing in the same year as the preceding, and of a similar import, was the publication *Social Dialects and Language Learning* (Shuy, ed., 1966) in which also appeared a contribution on the Jamaican situation (Bailey 1964).

It has already been shown in section three of this article that the community attitudes responsible for the failure of dialect readers in some parts of the United States of America are similar to the West

Indian attitudes that made it impracticable for the vernacular to be used as the language of instruction in schools; and in the studies just mentioned the recognition of the similarity of the second-dialect characteristics of the language situations in the U.S.A. and the West Indies has also been cited. This basic similarity between the two situations means that much of the work done in any one is likely to have some relevance for the other. In this respect, work such as that of Labov (1964; *et al.* 1965, 1966, 1969), Shuy (*et al.* 1967), Wolfram (1969), and Fasold and Shuy (eds., 1970), which provides structural descriptions of language variation and of non-Standard speech in the U.S.A., and which suggests ways in which such descriptions need to be taken into account in school programs, gives an example of the kinds of factors that also apply in the West Indies; similarly, work on the teaching of reading in the context of non-Standard speech, like that of Baratz and Shuy (1969) have a corresponding import. In some instances, researches have been done expressly with both the American and West Indian situations in mind; this is the case, for example, in Shuy (1972) which discusses strategies for implementing sociolinguistic principles in schools and DeCamp (1972) which examines problems and possibilities in the use of Standard English books by Creole-speaking children.

In all of the work referred to in the present section of this article, as pointed out already, mention is made of the possibilities of using foreign-language teaching methods in the essentially bidialectal educational situations of the United States of America and the West Indies. In some cases, as in Stewart (1964), mention is also made of the fact that, to the relevant learners, Standard English is neither a native nor a foreign language. For a long time after the first proposals for the use of foreign-language teaching methods in the relevant situations, however, there were no clear statements of the adaptations that inevitably became necessary because the native language of the learner overlapped considerably with the target, and because also, particularly in the West Indian situation, most non-Standard speakers were capable of varying their performance along a stretch of the Creole/Standard continuum. The methods that were advocated varied from a formal English-as-a-second-language programme, with a strictly ordered set of procedures based on contrasts between English and the basilect, to the almost informal and fortuitous counselling described by Brooks (1964):

... A trained volunteer now works with Carlos, often in this way. The boy picks up an interesting picture.
"I hab a tree, with leebs", says Carlos.

"Yes, you *have* a tree, with *leaves*", replies the teacher. "Say *have – leaves*".

"*Have – leaves*" replies Carlos, learning the /v/ sound in English. Because this boy already knows some English, he needs mainly to have someone take an interest in him to draw out what he knows, to involve him in the life around him, to help him share with others – orally and in writing – his valuable contributions, and *to correct some speech difficulties.*

The differences in the emphasis and focus of the various suggested applications of foreign-language teaching procedures are such that it would obviously be beneficial to have some clear theory of the relationship between foreign language teaching and what is essentially second dialect teaching. In the West Indies, the first teaching experiment aiming at some formalization of the new methodology began in Jamaica in 1965 and has been described in Craig (1969). Some theoretical principles underlying the methodology itself have been discussed in Craig (1966a and b, 1967, 1971a). In these studies it is shown that in a bidialectal situation of the kind relevant here, the learning of the new dialect proceeds as a mixing of newly learned linguistic features with older ones not yet replaced, so that in the case of the non-Standard speaker, the growing Standard repertoire that is being learned never appears separate and distinct until after prolonged learning when the acquisition of the Standard is quite complete. At each intermediate point of learning, the Standard tends to be produced mixed with survivals of the original non-Standard dialect. This does not mean that the speaker necessarily loses his original Creole or dialect, although this could happen with prolonged immersion into the cultural environment of the (high-prestige) Standard speech; but what happens is that the speaker acquires the ability to shift his speech closer to the Standard-language end of the Creole/Standard or dialect continuum; in other words, learning of the standard proceeds as a movement along this continuum.

In some cases during the acquisition of the Standard, a continuum can actually be seen in creation where none existed before, or rather, where no continuum items of a particular kind existed before. This was noticed, for example, in some of the children (7–8 years old) considered in the teaching experiment and related studies last referred to. Before these children became subjects of a modified second-language teaching program, they did not possess "is" and "has", and for the latter mentioned they used only the uninflected form of the verb "have". After a period of learning "is" both as a copula and as AUX + "ing"-form, and before they learned to use "has", they regularly produced "is have" wherever "has" would have been appropriate. This habit passed away naturally, and without any special corrective, after the children learned to use "has".

Linked to the tendency of the children here being considered to mix newly acquired forms with their original language, to proceed in this way along the dialect or Creole/Standard continuum, and even to create a new continuum, was the ability to comprehend much more Standard language than they could produce. Wolfram (1970: 17) points out that such ability seems consistent with the viewpoint of Labov and Cohen (1967) that the main differences between non-Standard and Standard language appear to be on the surface rather than on the underlying levels of language; Labov himself (1969: 24) refers to such ability as having been significantly proved by repetition tests given to subjects in some of his earlier researches; and Baratz (1969) found similarly through subsequent tests of the same kind in her own work. What is most significant in the Labov and Baratz evidence is that the non-Standard speakers, while being unable themselves to produce the Standard language, were able to restructure that language in non-Standard equivalents, showing indeed that it was the underlying structure that must have been comprehended.

These indications in the children in the West Indian experiment confirmed a basic principle that directed the teaching methodology. This principle was that, as far as the learner was concerned, the continuum between Creole and Standard consisted of four hierarchical strata of linguistic structures as follows: A, those common to both Standard and non-Standard speech and therefore within the production repertoire of the learner; B, those not usually produced in the informal, non-Standard speech of the learner, but known to him and produced under stress in prestige social situations; C, those which the learner would recognise and comprehend if used by other speakers (especially in a meaningful context), but which the learner himself would be unable to produce; and D, those totally unknown to the learner. As will be shown subsequently, it is sometimes convenient to regard elements of strata A and B as forming a single class, and similarly, those of C and D as forming a single class; but even when regarded in this way the four underlying strata show that in the class of second-dialect language known already to the learner, there is a set of items which he would use only in unusual or very formal situations, and in the class of second-dialect language not within the production repertoire of the learner, there is a set of items which can be recognised and comprehended.

The special implications of this stratification of language vis-à-vis the Creole or non-Standard learner of English has been discussed in

Craig (1971: 378) where it is shown that, because of the B and C strata, the learner often fails to perceive new target D elements in the teaching situation, unlike the learner of a foreign language. Consequent upon this, the reinforcement of learning which derives from the learner's satisfaction at mastering a new element, and knowing he has mastered it, is minimal, unlike that accruing to the learner of a foreign language; and because of the ease of shifting from Standard English to Creole or other non-Standard speech and vice-versa, the learner, again unlike the learner of a foreign language, resists any attempt to restrict his use of language exclusively within the new language elements being taught to him.

In the light of these implications, it is not surprising if many non-Standard speakers taught by foreign language methods continue to show a very low rate of acquiring Standard language. Kochman (1969: 87) in discussing this point, felt that the "efficiency quotient" of Standard language teaching, i.e., the result that comes from an input of time and effort, is so negligible that the wisdom of at all attempting to teach the Standard under conditions such as those relevant here has to be questioned. Usually, the reasons for such poor results have been ascribed completely to social factors and the unfavorable attitudes of learners as in, for example, Fasold (1968) and Abrahams (1970). There is no doubt that social and attitudinal factors are exceedingly important and obviously play a part, but slow or negligible acquisition of the Standard is not restricted to poorly motivated learners or to learners below the age of social awareness (vide Labov 1964: 91) at which some motivation might develop. The question therefore needs to be studied of whether the very nature of bidialectal situations does not produce strictly linguistic and non-attitudinal factors that have some additional bearing on the poor results of language teaching.

The teaching program dictated by the suggested stratification of language, vis-à-vis the learner, and by the considerations related to that stratification is structured as follows:

1. Topics for treatment in language are selected so as to reflect the interests, maturity and immediate cultural environment of the learners, but at the same time so as to permit adequate use of the specific linguistic structures that form the goal of teaching at the specific point in time.

2. The learners are led by the teacher to explore the topic fully in whatever language the learners possess. The teacher may either speak the vernacular, or speak some other type of language closer to the Standard or speak the Standard itself, so long as the learners are able to

comprehend easily; and the teacher accepts whatever language the learners choose to respond in, including such new language as is infiltrating into the learners' competence. This part of the program is completely oral and may be designated "free talk". The purpose of this part is to promote normal growth and development of the learners in whatever language medium is most natural to them.

3.   The teacher uses the selected topic, or aspects of the topic, as the basis of systematic quasi-foreign language practice. Because of the high rate of recognition and comprehension in the bidialectal situation, through the learners possession of the language strata A, B, and C, teaching procedures do not usually call for a very intensive use of imitation drills, but rather more for substitution and transformation practices, controlled dialogues and dramas, and a heavy reliance on simulated situations for forcing learners into a creative use of the specific linguistic structures that are aimed at. This part of the program may be designated "controlled talk" and only Standard language is used.

4.   For teaching in (3) preceding, linguistic structures are selected so that, relevant to the A, B, C, D classification of structures already discussed, the learners are forced to use a target structure or target structures selected from C or D (which for practical purposes may be combined into a single class), and at the same time to use incidental structures which come fortuitously from A and B (which, again for practical purposes, may also be combined into a single class).

5.   Language learners who are also learning to read use material consisting only of such linguistic structures as at each given stage they have already learned as at (3), and that are relevant to the topics discussed at (2). Language learners who can already read may use materials that are linguistically unstructured (and the more such learners can be saturated with reading, the better). The purpose of this set of measures is to ensure that the acquisition of and interest in reading is not hampered by Standard-language deficiencies, and that reading and language-learning should reinforce each other; once reading is firmly acquired, however, there is no longer any point in linking it to the formal learning of language structure.

6.   For all learners, use is made in writing only of those linguistic structures that have already been learned as at (3), and in most cases the content of the writing is restricted to topics treated as at (2). By this means, writing is closely linked to proficiency in speech, and one reinforces the other.

7.   The various subject-areas of the total school curriculum enter into the selection of topics explained as at (1) so that aspects of these areas

get re-worked in controlled speech, reading and writing in the same way as all other experiences.

The difference between what is outlined here and strictly foreign-language teaching procedures lies in what has been termed free talk and the way in which controlled talk, reading and writing are linked to it and to one another; the different parts of the program have to be planned together and be well integrated. In this way, the learner gets the kind of stimulating education that ought to be present in a first-language prog-ramme, but at the same time, linked to this stimulation and arising out of it, there is a concentration on the ordered and sequenced teaching of new language elements. The built-in resistance of the second-dialect learner to such teaching is countered by the carry-over of his free-talk interests into other activities, by the constant reinforcement passing from one activity to another, and by the encouraged possibility of newly learned language gradually infiltrating into free talk, becoming a part of it and becoming gradually augmented. This last mentioned possibility is in fact more than just a possibility since it has been shown, as already discussed, to be the inevitable way in which language learning proceeds in this situation, i.e., as a gradual mixture and replacement of items along the continuum. This mixture and replacement occasioned by new lan-guage learning, as explained already, does not mean that the learners lose their original vernacular. They retain their original vernacular for such occasions as it is needed in their home and peer-group environment, but at the same time they acquire an increasing ability to shift their formal speech into the Standard-language end of the continuum until they achieve some acceptable proficiency in Standard speech. On the way towards the achievement of such proficiency, many compromises are inevitable: some learners might persist in retaining certain of their original speech characteristics in the most nearly Standard language they learn to produce, others might achieve good native proficiency in reading and writing the Standard language but at the same time persist in their original non-Standard speech even on the most formal occasions, and so on. It does not seem that bidialectal education ought to expect more than this. Fishman and Lueders-Salmon (1972) have shown that German dialect speakers react to the necessity as well as the experience of learning High German in some of the characteristic ways that are now well known in the United States of America and the West Indian language situations. It would thus seem that the factors discussed here are to be found universally in many different bidialectal situations.

The principles and procedures sketched in the preceding paragraphs will not be found in uniform application in schools within the West Indies. In Jamaica, where the educational principles just discussed were first and still are being worked out, indications of the methodology will be noticed in Ministry of Education school syllabuses and guidelines for teachers where "an integrated approach" to language teaching is spoken of; the "integration" involves the components of the programme already outlined here. At the present time, an effort is being made in the Ministry's Curriculum Development Thrust to supply teachers with detailed guides and materials for teaching along the suggested lines. The ideas and procedures are also in process of being disseminated through others of the officially English-speaking West Indian territories; in Guyana, for example, much consideration has been given to the nature of the Guyanese language situation and the needs that exist in education. The discussion has proceded very much along the general lines follow-ed in this chapter, and some of it is exampled in Tyndal (1965, 1972), Armstrong (1968), Wilson (1968), Cave (1970, 1971), Craig (1971), and Trotman (1973). In the last mentioned territory also, the production of classroom materials incorporating the relevant procedures is in progress.

In the Eastern Caribbean, independently of the Jamaica-based work, the School of Education of the University of The West Indies together with a UNESCO curriculum development program in that area has been working on the development of language-teaching materials with an English-as-a-second language approach. Preceding this development and continuing concurrently with it, there is in Trinidad an ongoing survey of school-children's language (Carrington and Borely 1969); there has also been concluded a survey of teaching practices (Carrington, Borely, and Knight (1972), textbooks in use in schools (Knight, Carring-ton, and Borely 1972), and the home-language background of Trinidad children (Carrington, Borely, and Knight 1972a); the latter collections of information are considered as a preliminary to the development of teaching procedures in that territory.

No matter what stage of development has been reached at present in the development of bidialectal educational procedures in the relevant individual West Indian territories, however, it seems quite clear that, in the long run, the fact that such procedures are necessary and are at the same time inevitably different from both native and foreign-language teaching procedures will have to be faced; it seems important that when this happens, the principles and procedures discussed above should be available for more extensive trial throughout the region.

6. LANGUAGE AND SOCIAL CLASS IN A BIDIALECTAL SITUATION

The speakers of Creole or non-Standard language are invariably of low social status, therefore, in bidialectal situations of the kind relevant here, the problems of educating such speakers are very much the problems of educating economically depressed and low-status persons in a socially stratified society. Since the 1960's particularly, there has been considerable discussion of the relationships between social class, language, mental ability, and education. Much of this discussion is as relevant to bidialectal education in the West Indies as it is to similar situations elsewhere, and it has been found essential that the planning of West Indian school programmes should take note of it.

By far the most important aspect of this discussion is that which emerged out of work like that of Reissman (1962) in the United States of America and Bernstein (1961a, b, c; 1962a, b; 1965, 1966) in Britain. The former expanded on the thesis of the limited mental and learning capacities of the "culturally deprived child"; the latter, actually preceding this in point of time, gave an apparently rational basis for this thesis by suggesting that the different patterns of socialization in lower and upper social-class environments gave rise respectively to restricted and elaborated linguistic codes, the latter code indicating a "more extensive and qualitatively different order of verbal planning" as compared with the former. The 1961 and 1962 work of Bernstein states the objective linguistic characteristics of these codes and shows that restricted code users, of low social class as predicted, are generally lower in measured intelligence and educational achievement than elaborated code users who, as predicted, are mostly found in the upper social class. The remainder of this work that followed in the later 1960's stressed the socialization factor somewhat more and showed that it was possible for both codes to arise in any social class depending on the conditioning received by subjects; but in any case, the dominant social-class pattern was still that demonstrated in the earlier work. The Bernstein thesis has received general support in the work of Lawton (1963, 1964, 1968), Robinson (1965; *et al.* 1968), Coulthard (*et al.* 1968), Hawkins (1969) as well as elsewhere; the main additional fact emerging from these researches is that low social-class subjects, influenced by education, sometimes have an elaborated code available for selected purposes; but this does not alter the main thesis that on the whole, the lower social class is habituated in a mode of language use that puts it at a disadvantage in the performance of certain linguistic and intellectual operations.

This viewpoint of low-social-class disabilities was firmly accepted in most educational programmes of the 1960's that have had to deal with social-class or cultural extremes. It is well exemplified in writings such as those of Corbin (*et al.* 1965), Crow (*et al.* 1966) and Bereiter (*et al.* 1966) which have had a wide influence on early educational practices not only in the United States of America but elsewhere. The main opposition to this viewpoint has come from sociolinguists; Labov (*et al.* 1965, 1969), for example, has shown that lower-social-class language in natural and uninhibiting circumstances is accompanied by much creativity and efficiency in the treatment of logical relationships and the processing of ideas. It is shown on the other hand that the expression of meaning in upper-social-class language can often be accompanied by much vagueness, empty verbosity and a lack of conciseness. It is also shown that the contexts in which upper- and lower-social-class children are studied: classroom-type situations and topics, talking about pictures, obviously upper-class interviewers and testers, and so on, militate against lower-social-class children who cannot help but be uncomfortable and anxious in such contexts, and who are thereby induced to minimize their language production.

But so far, apart from questioning the circumstances under which language-data is obtained in social-class comparisons, (although Labov (ibid.) did make an additional argument which will be further considered subsequently) arguments for the basic equality of language capabilities between social classes have been based mainly on the concept of the equality of linguistic competence. However, the acceptance of this concept as a true representation of reality does not rule out the possibility that the habitual linguistic performances required in opposed social-class environments and situations might differ so considerably as to impose habitually different language-behavioral capabilities on lower and upper-social-class speakers. It seems to be the latter possibility that is suggested within the thesis of lower-social-class language disabilities; Bernstein (1972) if not before, states this very clearly. In order to argue successfully against such a thesis, the contention that lower-social-class language systems, as such, have a potential equal to that of any other natural language systems is not sufficient; there would additionally need to be a valid demonstration that there is no difference in the kinds of language performances that are habitual at social-class extremes. If there are no habitual performance differences, then obviously the questions being discussed here would be fictitious ones created out of the misrepresentation of lower-social-class behavior. If there are habitual performance differences, then this still would not in itself mean that the incidence of any specific performance characteristics is or is not responsible for specific abilities or disabilities of an intellectual kind. And finally, even if it should be shown that some performance characteristics are indeed to be associated with specific intellectual abilities or disabilities, this would still be far removed from the position of Jensen (1969), Eynsenck (1971) and others against whom the LSA resolution on language equality (LSA Bulletin, March 1972) argued, since there would be no need to assume an hereditary factor (or a racial factor) and to ignore, as Jensen and others do, the obvious sociological explanations that would be apparent for such abilities or disabilities. Apart, therefore, from the question of the equality of linguistic competence (which seems adequately answered in the Labov and LSA references already cited) there are two issues to be examined. One is whether specific language characteristics do at all indicate specific intellectual abilities or disabilities; the other is whether habitual linguistic performances differ in different social-class environments, and if they do, in what ways and with what results.

The evidence so far presented that specific language characteristics indicate specific intellectual abilities or disabilities consists entirely of correlations between such language characteristics on the one hand and social class, measured intelligence and educational achievement on the other. Measured intelligence and educational achievement have long been shown to be determined by environment, and to be biased towards middle and upper-class norms because, inevitably, of the way in which the measuring instruments have to be (or have been) constructed and administered. Some of the relevant researches are Nisbet (1953), Ferguson (1954), Floud and Halsey (1957), Vernon (1955, 1965a and b, 1966, 1967), Bruner (*et al.* 1956, 1966), McClelland (*et al.* 1953, 1958, 1961), Douglas (1964), John (1962), Klein (1965), Goodnow (1968). It is therefore not surprising if the characteristics of low-social-class language correlate negatively with measured intelligence and educational achievement, while those of upper-social-class language do the opposite. Consequently, information about correlations between language characteristics and intelligence or achievement measurements cannot at this stage answer the question of whether specific language characteristics are responsible for specific abilities or disabilities. The nearest possible approach to an answer can come only from an examination of the language characteristics themselves that are in question, and an analysis of the cognitive tasks they actually permit speakers to perform or not to perform.

Essentially, in a very preliminary and anecdotal way, such an examination and analysis was attempted in Labov (1969), but the full range of language characteristics, their possible interrelationships and their total communication implications are yet to be studied. The specific language characteristics in question, cited as demonstrating social-class differences in language-related abilities, are as follows:

(a)   Vocabulary as measured by the presence of higher-order lexical categories and proportions of types to tokens.
(b)   Length of sentences or clauses or minimally terminable syntactic units (T units as in Loban [1963]).
(c)   Complexity as measured by quantities of dependent clauses as a whole, or specific types of dependent clauses involving logical relationships.
(d)   The occurrence of various phrase-types, including nominalizations or nominal groups that are in the nature of reduced sentences.
(e)   The frequency of use of adjectives, or adjective-type modification.

In Craig (1971a: 382–5), it was pointed out, that in terms of language characteristics such as these, West Indian Creole speech would have to be regarded as a Bernstein type of restricted code, but that at the same time Creole speakers who had begun to learn Standard English and to shift their speech progressively towards the Standard end of the continuum seemed, in terms of the same characteristics, to be acquiring an elaborated code. It was further pointed out that this phenomenon, in relation to codal differences, implied a contradiction in terms, since such differences should not be merely functions of different morpho-syntactic systems and be variable in the way they appear to be in the Creole/Standard English continuum. What seemed to be indicated here was that at the Creole or non-Standard end of the continuum there was a certain style of communication which produced the morpho-syntactic characteristics commonly taken as evidence of restricted coding, while at the Standard end of the continuum the communication style was different and resulted in the opposite characteristics. This difference in communication styles carried with it no evidence that the content of language, or the content that could possibly be treated in the two styles of language, was any different.

These indications were confirmed in a study of the use of language in young Jamaican children living in contrasting socio-economic environments (Craig 1971b), and some implications of this confirmation have been discussed in Craig (1972, 1973). In this work it was shown, by comparisons of the types of language characteristics set out in sets (a) to (e) one paragraph ago, and by comparison also of the total volume of language produced in a given time, that different communication styles were evident at opposite extremes of the continuum and that these styles had the following objective results, *given the same set of meanings at each end.*

At the Creole or non-Standard extreme: More basic sentence-forms and relationships, consequently shorter sentences, and also consequently more numerous sentences per given quantity of words. Concrete nominal and more direct verbal vocabulary. Less adjectives as a whole, but with verbs often doing the work of adjectives, since shorter and more numerous sentences permitted a relatively larger quantity of main verbs; for this same reason, less of some transformationally derived lexical subcategories and less diversity of vocabulary. A larger absolute quantity of words per unit of time, probably attributable to the fact that this communication style requires less complex internal organization before an output of language is made.

At the Standard extreme: Less basic and more transformationally derived sentence-forms and relationships, consequently longer sentences and also consequently less sentences per given quantity of words. More vocabulary items that are non-concrete, generalized and transformationally derived. More adjectives as a whole, especially such adjectives as provide generalized labels for sets of behavioral characteristics that might otherwise be represented as strings of short verb-phrases; consequently greater diversity of vocabulary. A smaller absolute quantity of words per unit of time, probably attributable to the fact that this communication style requires a more complex internal organization before an output of language is made.

In effect, the characteristics of the two styles accrue from the cumulative results of Creole and Standard sentences like the respectively (a) and (b) examples which follow and, which are meaning equivalents in each case, though not morpho-syntactically alike.

1. (a) / im tel lai an tiif /
       him tell lie and him thief (i.e., "steals")
   (b) He is untrustworthy.

2. (a)   / im laik waak bout an taak-taak wen im fi wok /
          him like walk about and talk-talk when him (ought) to work.
    (b)   He likes to idle. Or: He is idlesome.
3. (a)   / im na wier shuu, an im wok plenti moni /
          him not wear shoe, and him work plenty money.
    (b)   He doesn't wear shoes although he earns much money.
4. (a)   / im tek stuon hit di guot ina im ed, an di guot ded /
          him take stone hit the goat in him head, and the goat dead.
    (b)   He killed the goat by hitting it in its head with a stone.

From contrasts like those in (1) and (2) will come short, "and" – linked
sentences for the Creole or Non-standard speaker, while, for the Standard speaker, there will be none of these, but rather a single sentence with
more generalized vocabulary items, most likely adjectives. From contrasts like those in (3), "and" – linked sentences with the appropriate
intonation produced by the Creole or non-Standard speaker, would be
represented in the Standard speaker by main and subordinate clauses
with logical connectors and a more abstract vocabulary. From contrasts
like those in (4), the Standard speaker would obtain a single long sentence with transformationally derived phrases and vocabulary, while the
non-Standard speaker will produce several short sentences, sometimes
very loosely linked. But in each case, the underlying meanings being
mediated in the two styles would be the same.

The preceding are merely a few examples, obviously not intended to be
exhaustive; obviously too, there could be many other types of underlying
meaning equivalences that could be differently represented in the two
styles. It is also not the intention here to suggest that Creole or non-
Standard speakers produce all their sentences in the relevant exampled
style, and that Standard speakers always do correspondingly in their own
characteristic style. The two suggested styles are envisaged as dominant
characteristics at the respective social-class extremes, but it is to be
expected that there will be times when there might well be no difference
in styles over given stretches of actual speech at each social-class extreme.
In the actual Jamaican study already referred to, where the differences
between speakers are expressed in terms of the occurrence frequencies of
linguistic items, these points emerge relatively clearly.

What has been suggested here is that the language characteristics often
regarded as indicating intellectual abilities or disabilities in fact indicate
nothing more than contrasting styles of communication. A common set of
underlying meanings mediated in the two styles would have different
surface-level results. These surface-level results are in the nature of habits

that can be learned automatically as a natural part of the process of learning a Standard dialect; this explains why such learning not only results in a movement along the Creole or dialect continuum but appears also as a change from restricted to elaborated coding in terms of the characteristics so far suggested for these codes. There is no reason to suppose that the factors discussed here relevant to the Jamaican situation do not, at least in some measure, apply in other essentially bidialectal situations. The realities of dialect or quasi-dialect differences have generally been ignored in the whole theory of restricted and elaborated coding, and even linguists who have always been aware of these realities have often erred by forgetting that the use of language always involves certain communication characteristics not so far described or describable in the orthodox formulations of phonology and grammar.

The question of the results of habit-formation through the constant use of a particular communication style, and constant involvement in a particular set of environmentally determined language-purposes and language-content characteristics, now deserves some attention.

It should not be surprising if speakers who are habituated in a particular communication style find it relatively more difficult to comprehend discourse in a style different from their own, even if phonology and grammar are held constant. When once the differently styled discourse is comprehended however, the relevant speakers would have no problem in reconstructing the discourse in their own particular style, even though they would be unable to reproduce it in the style in which they originally received it; that a capability similar to this exists in non-Standard speakers, and the implications of it, have been mentioned already as being illustrated in the work of Labov and Baratz earlier referred to in this section of the chapter. It is to be expected therefore that lower-social-class speakers would tend to find it relatively difficult to comprehend the dominant Standard-language communication style, while upper-social-class speakers would tend to find the opposite. It is also possible that lower-social-class speakers might acquire the phonology and grammar of Standard speech, while at the same time retaining the lower-social-class communication style and using it on most occasions, except when specially motivated to select the other style. This would explain the findings of later researches in the Bernstein group that lower social-class children often have an elaborated code available. The matter, however, probably goes further than this.

It is well known, from work such as that of Luria and Yodovich (1959), Luria (1961), and Vygotsky (1962), that the possession of appropriate language facilitates the performance of many types of cognitive task

many of which are ostensibly non-verbal; and it seems that many of the
tasks required of school children are of the latter kind. Much more
investigation needs to be done in this area, but it seems quite possible
that the aspects of language that might be most facilitating in this way
have to do with the availability of appropriate lexical labels for the
specific percepts and relationships being dealt with, since the possession
of an ability to use a label implies some prior mental acquaintance with
and orientation towards the relevant experience. It is consequently
possible that the communication style and the language system linked to
it at the Standard-language extreme might possess a larger repertoire of
such facilitating lexical labels particularly in relation to cognitive tasks
that are most relevant, in any case, to the upper-social-class subculture.
If this is the case, then the habitual user of such a style might have some
advantage over users of the opposite style in the performance of certain
tasks required in conventional education, performance in intelligence
and achievement tests, and so on. At the same time, it is also quite possible
that there are special characteristics of the Creole or non-Standard
communication style and its own language system that might well
facilitate the performance of other kinds of tasks. It is possible, for example, that the dominance in this style of short, basic NP + VP combinations,
very directly related to experience, might well be related to the superiority displayed in imaginative activity by the lower-social-status children
studied by Geoffrey Turner (described in Bernstein 1972: 142); and there
could possibly be other activities in which this particular communicative
style might be more facilitating than the opposite style is.

The position taken here, and justified in the Jamaican study already
cited, differs from that of Bernstein because the mentioned communication styles are regarded as contingent characteristics of respectively
different morpho-syntactic systems, in such a way that the learning of
one system confers the respective style, so long as that one system is
being used without interference from the other. In this respect, the two
types of communication are in a relation similar to that of two discrete
natural languages; it might be easier to say certain things in one language
than it is in the other, but the natural users of the two languages have the
same cognitive and intellectual competence, and no one set of users
possesses any absolute cognitive abilities or disabilities different from
those of the other.

Apart from what has here been referred to as communication style
and its usually contingent morpho-syntax, another aspect of language in
which constant, socially determined habituation might possibly produce

some cognitive result is the purposes, aims, and intentions with which language is used. It should not be surprising if social-class extremes differ in the detailed emphasis put upon such purposes, aims, and intentions; such differences, with reference to whole cultures and subcultures have been the burden of ethnographic studies from Malinowski (1923) to, for example, Hymes (1961a and b, 1962) and much of Gumperz and Hymes (1972). This aspect of the use of language would be reflected objectively in the narrow types of performative and illocutionary acts, in the sense of Austin (1962) and Searle (1969) that speakers are habituated to carry out in language; this aspect, it is important to note, could not possibly be revealed by the kinds of language characteristics (*a* to *e* earlier exampled) often examined in studies of social-class differences. In the Jamaican study relevant here, it was found that lower-social-class children talking freely among themselves tended to engage in conversational exchanges involving questions, exclamations, commands, and various types of interpersonal adjustments more frequently than upper-social-class children did in similar circumstances. At first (e.g., Craig 1971b: 346–7) this indication seemed to agree with the Bernstein prediction that children of this social class would be more strongly habituated than upper-social-class children towards communicating in shared referential situations, communicating for very pragmatic purposes, and so on. Subsequent consideration of the data has placed a reservation on this indication, which is that this trait of the children does not imply any "restriction" in the Bernstein sense, relative to their upper-social-class counterparts, but implies rather a relatively greater interest in their peers and in personal relationships. This conclusion seems supported by other evidence which will be mentioned subsequently.

The remaining aspects of language use in which specific constant habituation might have some determining effect on cognitive abilities may all be subsumed under the label: "content" of language; content in this sense refers to the objects, experiences and relationships that are treated in language. Differences in this aspect of language, if they exist, ought to be reflected objectively in the narrow semantic subclasses of grammatical categories and contextual assumptions that speakers are accustomed to communicate. In the study of Jamaican children here being referred to, lower-social-class children referenced persons, including adults, far more frequently than upper-social-class children did; this trait fitted well with the predominant interest of the former children, already referred to above, in interpersonal relationships. In traits such as egocentricity (commonly referred to in earlier codal studies) rural children showed the greater tendency and no appreciable absolute difference between upper and lower-social-class urban children was shown. Lower-social-class children showed a stronger tendency than upper-social-class children did to reference the present and immediate in both place and time. This is in accord with the prediction of the Bernstein theory, but here again a reservation (not as clearly evidenced in Craig 1971b, for example) has to be placed on the possible interpretation, since the children would in any case be obliged to make such references because of their already mentioned interests in their peers, in persons generally and in what usually happened immediately around them. The parallel upper-social-class interest on the other hand, tended to be more anecdotal, referring more often to what the children had been told, or learnt at second hand or to what happened once, as distinct from what usually happens. Lower-social-class children referenced concepts of number, sequencing, and obligation (in modal verbs) more frequently than their upper-social-class counterparts did, but the latter referenced probability and possibility more frequently than the former. Causal, conditional, and concessive relationships did not discriminate strongly between the different sets of children, but upper-social-class boys made references to such concepts less than other children did. Altogether, these apparently habitual differences in the content of language seem strongly related to the dominant interests, types of relationships, and experiences that could naturally be expected in the contrasting social environments. There is no evidence that this kind of habituation in content would lead to any absolute cognitive abilities or disabilities.

The total evidence on social-class influences relevant to the language abilities of Jamaican children may be summarized as follows: most of the social-class language differences commonly referred to by previous researchers are differences in communication styles that have nothing to do with cognitive abilities, and that can be acquired with the learning of the specific morpho-syntactic systems to which they are related; differences in the purposes and content of language can inevitably be expected to appear and to differentiate between persons existing in different cultural environments, since the interrelationships between speakers, and the interests and life experiences of speakers can be expected to differ with environments. There is no evidence that habituation in specific styles, sets of language purposes and types of content create any absolute cognitive abilities or disabilities, but it does seem that many of the performances, including linguistic ones, required in conventional education are present more frequently, and can therefore be more easily learned, in upper-social-class than in lower-social-class environments. There are still some performances, however, that do seem to be facilitated by the lower-social-class experience. What most often happens in education is that the child of lower-social-class is often required to acquire certain learned responses which come naturally only in the upper-social-class environment; on the other hand no corresponding requirement is necessary that the upper-social-class child should acquire learned lower-social-class responses. The factors that have been considered here with special reference to the Jamaican situation seem to have relevance for all bidialectal or quasi-bidialectal situations in the West Indies as well as elsewhere.

One of the most important practical implications of the preceding is that the teaching of the Standard dialect also involves the teaching of a particular communication style. Some of the procedures that would need to be specially considered in such teaching are discussed in Craig (1972). The procedures involve taking what might otherwise be terminal Standard-language strings except for a lower-social-class communication style and learning to proceed through the transformations that would transform such strings into the opposite communication style. For the non-Standard speaker learning the Standard, this type of learning might not be crucial from the point of view of language production, but it certainly seems to have an important bearing on the reception of Standard language. Without such learning, many originally non-Standard speakers who succeed in mastering the basic morphology and syntax of the Standard operate at a relatively low receptive level, a fact which seldom becomes evidenced until such speakers begin to experience the demands of higher education.

7. THE TOTAL REQUIREMENTS OF EDUCATION: A SUMMARY

The increase, since the 1950's, of Creole language studies has brought with it an improved understanding of the sociolinguistic factors that operate in Creole or non-Standard dialect situations. In the West Indies, such situations are virtually bidialectal ones, as far as education is concerned, in the officially English-speaking territories. The situations bear some resemblance to the social-dialect or the lower-social-class ones in the United States of America and Britain, although social conditions and (especially in territories where there are strong survivals of basilect Creoles) linguistic ones too are often substantially different.

In the relevant territories, Standard English or a special variety of it is the language of education; and although Creole or post-Creole speech is often regarded as closely identified with the national consciousness and identity, and is preserved for close personal exchanges and the continued development of a vernacular culture, there does not seem to be any possibility, because of the dominant attitudes of the population, that such speech will be accepted as the official language or the language of education. In this context, schools are faced with the task of helping children to develop naturally and without inhibition in their home language, but at the same time to become fluent users of Standard speech.

Education authorities throughout the region recognize the need for a new approach to language education, so that the already stated task of schools might be achieved more efficiently than it has been in the past. However, especially in the context of economic underdevelopment and consequent scarcity of resources, educational innovations take a long time to reach the classroom; there are still classroom survivals of the procedure of teaching the Standard by correcting, and inhibiting the normal speech of children. Ideas of teaching the Standard by quasi-foreign language methods, have begun to make an impact, however, but even in the United States of America where such ideas have been most implemented, problems have been experienced and the returns of teaching are slow and small; similar problems are experienced in the West Indies, but the special procedures necessary for second-dialect teaching are being more carefully studied beginning with experiments in Jamaica; the results of the latter are being disseminated through other territories.

The total requirements of bidialectal education include much more than merely teaching the Standard dialect without inhibiting the child's home language. It includes a full utilization of the child's natural cultural environment, and at the same time it includes developing in the child the knowledge, skills, attitudes and cultural attributes necessary for mobility in the society as a whole. This total aim, when linked to the fundamental problem of language education, makes it imperative that the implications of relationships between language and other aspects of human behavior be taken into consideration in educational planning. The most important factor in this connection is the relationship between language and social class, since the Creole or post-Creole speakers in the West Indies is characteristically an individual of low social class, while the Standard language and most of the aims and content of conventional education are indigenous to the upper social class. Studies of this relationship, again beginning in Jamaica, question the theory of lower-social-class deficiency, but suggest that the acquisition of Standard language involves more than the acquisition of phonology, morphology, and syntax; the results of this seem important for second-dialect teaching.

University of West Indies,
Mona-Kingston, Jamaica

REFERENCES

Aarons, B., and Stewart, W. A. (eds.) (1969), "Linguistic-cultural differences and American education", *The Florida FL Reporter*, Anthology issue.
Abrahams, R. D. (1970), "The advantages of black English", Southern Conference of Language Learning, Florida 1970.
Alatis, J. W. (ed.) (1969), Twentieth Annual Round Table Meeting, Number 22. Georgetown University School of Linguistics.
Alleyne, M. C. (1961), "Communication and politics in Jamaica", *Caribbean Studies* 3.
— (1963), "Language and society in St. Lucia", *Caribbean Studies* 1 (1).
Allsopp, S. R. R. (1949–53), "The language we speak", *Kyk-over-all*, Vols. 2, 3, 5. Guyana.
— (1958a), "The English language in British Guiana", *English Language Teaching* 12 (2).
— (1958b), "Pronominal forms in the dialect of English used in Georgetown (British Guiana) and its environs by people engaged in non-clerical occupations". M. A. thesis. University of London.
— (1962), "Expression of state and action in the dialect of English used in the Georgetown area of British Guiana". Ph.D. dissertation. University of London.
— (1965), "British Honduras – The linguistic dilemma", *Caribbean Quarterly* 11 (3 and 4).
— (1972a), "Some suprasegmental features of Caribbean English".
— (1972b), "The problem of acceptability in Caribbean creolized English", in: *Creole Languages and Educational Development: Papers from the Conference Sponsored by UNESCO and UWI, July 1972*, ed. by D. R. Craig. To be published. London, New Beacon Publications.
Armstrong, B. (1968), "The teaching of English in Guiana", *The Guiana Teacher*, 2 (7).
Austin, J. L. (1962), *How To Do Things With Words*, ed. by J. O. Urmson. Harvard University Press.
Bailey, B. L. (1953), "Creole languages of the Caribbean area". M. A. thesis. Columbia University.
— (1962), *A Language Guide to Jamaica*. New York, Research Institute for the Study of Man.
— (1963), "Teaching of English noun-verb concord in primary schools in Jamaica", *Caribbean Quarterly*, 9 (4).
— (1964), "Some problems in the language teaching situation in Jamaica", in: *Social Dialects and Language Learning*, by Roger W. Shuy. Champaign, Illinois, National Council of Teachers of English.
— (1966), *Jamaican Creole Syntax: A Transformational Approach*. Cambridge University Press.
— (1971), "Jamaican creole: can dialect boundaries be defined?", in: Hymes (ed.).
Bailey, C. J. N. (1969–70), "Studies in three-dimensional language theory I–IV", *Working Papers in Linguistics*. University of Hawaii.

—   (1970), "Using data variation to confirm, rather than undermine, the validity of abstract syntactic structures", *Working Papers In Linguistics*. University of Hawaii.

Baratz, J. C. (1969), "Teaching Reading in an urban negro school system", in: Baratz and Shuy (eds.).

Baratz, J. and Shuy, R. W. (eds.) (1969), *Teaching Black Children to Read*. Washington, D.C., Center for Applied Linguistics.

Bennett, L. (1942), "Jamaica dialect verse: comp. George R. Bowen", *The Herald* Kingston.

—   (1943), *Jamaica Humour in Dialect*. Kingston, Gleaner Jamaica Press Association.

—   (1950), *Anancy Stories and Dialect Verse*. Kingston, Jamaica, Pioneer Press.

Bereiter *et al.* (1966), *Teaching Disadvantaged Children in the Preschool*. Englewood Cliffs, N. J., Prentice-Hall Inc.

Bernstein, B. (1961a), "Social structure, language and learning", *Educational Research* 3.

—   (1961b), "Social class and linguistic developments: a theory of social learning", in: *Economy, Education and Society*, ed. by A. H. Halsey, J. Floud and A. Anderson. New York, The Free Press.

—   (1961c), "Aspects of language and learning in the genesis of the social process", *Journal of Child Psychology and Psychiatry* 1:313. Reprinted, pp. 251–63 in: *Language, Culture and Society*, by D. Hymes.

—   (1962a), "Linguistic codes, hesitation phenomena are intelligence", *Language and Speech* 5:31–46.

—   (1962b), "Social class, linguistic codes and grammatical elements", *Language and Speech* 5:221–24.

—   (1965), "A socio-linguistic approach to social learning", in: *Social Science Survey*, ed. by J. Gould. London, Pelican.

—   (1966), "Elaborated and restricted codes: an outline", in: S. Lieberson (ed.).

—   (1972), "A critique of the concept of compensatory education", in: Cazden, John, and Hymes.

Berry, J. (1972), "Some observations on residual tone in West Indian English", in: Craig (ed.). To be published.

Bickerton, D. (1971), "Guyanese Speech". Manuscript. University of Guyana.

—   (1971a), "Inherent variability and variable rules", *Foundations of Language* 7.

—   (1972), "The structure of polyectal grammars", in: Shuy (ed.), 1973.

—   (1973), "On the nature of a creole continuum", *Language* 49 (3).

Brooks, C. K. (1964), "Some approaches to teaching English as a second language", in: Stewart (ed.).

Bronkhurst, H. V. P. (1888), *Among the Hindus and Creole of British Guiana*. London, T. Woolmar.

Bruner *et al.* (1956), *A Study of Thinking*. London, Chapman & Hall.

—   (1966), *Studies in Cognitive Growth*. New York, Wiley.

Bull, W. E. (1955), "Review of: The use of vernacular languages in education", *IJAL* 21:288–94.

Carrington, L. D. (1967), "St. Lucia Creole: A descriptive analysis of its phonology and morphosyntax". Ph.D. dissertation. Mona, University of the West Indies.

—   (1968), "English language learning problems in the Caribbean", *Trinidad and Tobago Modern Language Review* No. 1.

—   (1969), "Deviations from standard English in the speech of primary school children in St. Lucia and Dominica", *IRAL*, Vol. VIII/3.

—   (1970), "English language teaching in the Commonwealth Caribbean", *Commonwealth Education Liaison Committee Newsletter* 2 (10).

Carrington, L. D., and Borely, C. (1969), "An investigation into English language learning and teaching problems in Trinidad and Tobago". Mimeographed, St. Augustine, UWI Institute of Education.

Carrington, L. D., Borely, C., and Knight, E. H. (1972), *Away Robin Run: A Critical Description of the Teaching of the Language Arts in the Primary Schools of Trinidad and Tobago*. St. Augustine, Trinidad, Institute of Education.

— (1972a), *Linguistic exposure of Trinidad children*. St. Augustine, Trinidad. Institute of Education.

Carroll, J. B. (1960), "Language development in children", in: Saporta (ed.), 1961.

Cassidy, F. G. (1961), *Jamaica Talk: Three Hundred Years of the English Language in Jamaica*. London, Macmillan.

Cassidy, F. G., and LePage, R. B. (1967), *Dictionary of Jamaica English*. Cambridge University Press.

— (1972), "Jamaican creole and Twi: some comparisons", in: Craig (ed.), to be published.

Cave, G. N. (1970), "Sociolinguistic factors in Guyana language", *Language Learning* 20 (2).

— (1971), *Primary School Language in Guyana*, Georgetown, Guyana Teachers' Association.

— (1972), "Measuring linguistic maturity: the case of the noun stream", in: Craig (ed.), to be published.

Cazden, C. B., John, V. P., and Hymes, D. (eds.) (1972), *Functions of Language in the Classroom*. New York, Columbia University, Teachers College Press.

Christie, P. (1969), "A sociolinguistic study of some Dominican creole speakers". Ph.D. dissertation. University of York.

Collymore, Frank (ed.) (1952 onwards), *Bim*. Barbados, Advocate Press.

Corbin, R., and Crosby, M. (1965), *Language Programs for the Disadvantaged*. Champaign, Illinois, NCTE.

Coulthard *et al.* (1968), "The structure of the nominal group and elaboratedness of code", *Language and Speech* 11 (2):234–50.

Craig, D. R. (1964), "The written English of some 14-year-old Jamaican and English children" in: *Faculty of Education*. U.W.I.

— (1966a), "Some developments in language teaching in the West Indies", *Caribbean Quarterly*, 12 (1).

— (1966b), "Teaching English to Jamaican creole speakers: A model of a multi-dialect situation", *Language Learning* 16 (1–2).

— (1967), "Some early indications of learning a second dialect", *Language Learning* 17 (3 and 4).

— (1969), *An Experiment in Teaching English*. Caribbean University Press and London, Ginn and Co., Ltd.

— (1971), "English in Secondary Education in a former British Colony: a case study of Guyana", *Caribbean Studies* 10 (4).

— (1971a), "Education and creole English in the West Indies: some sociolinguistic factors", in: Hymes (ed.), 1971.

— (1971b), "The use of language by 7-year old Jamaican children living in contrasting socio-economic environments. Unpublished Ph.D. thesis. University of London.

— (1972), "Intralingual differences, communication and language theory", in: Craig (ed.), forthcoming.

— (1973), "Social class, language and communication in Jamaican children", in: *Education in the Commonwealth* 6. London, Commonwealth Secretariat.

— (Forthcoming) *Creole Languages and Educational Development: Papers from the Conference Sponsored by UNESCO and the UWI, July 1972*. London, New Beacon Publications.

Crow, L. D., *et al.* (1966), *Educating the Culturally Disadvantaged Child*. New York, David Mckay Co.

Cruickshank, J. G. (1911), "Negro English with reference particularly to Barbados", *Timehri*, 3rd series, 1 (183).
— (1916), *"Black talk". Being notes on negro dialect in British Guiana with (inevitably) a chapter on the vernacular of Barbados*. Guiana, The Argosy Press.
Cuffie, D. (1964), "Problems in the teaching of English in the island of Trinidad from 1797 to the present day". M.A. Thesis. University of London, Institute of Education.
DeCamp, D. (1971), "Toward a generative analysis of a post creole speech continuum", in: Hymes (ed.), 1971.
— (1972), "Standard English books and creole speaking children", in: Craig (ed.), forthcoming.
Douglas, J. W. B. (1964), *The home and the School*. London and New York, MacGibbon and Kee.
Edwards, W. (1972), "'Have' and 'be' in Guyanese creole", in: Graig (ed.), forthcoming.
Eysenck, H. J. (1971), *Race, Intelligence and Education*. London, Temple Smith.
Faculty of Education, University of the West Indies. (1965), "Language teaching, linguistics and the teaching of English in a multilingual society", *Report of the Conference at University of The West Indies, April 1964*.
Fasold, R. W. (1968), "Isn't English the first language too?", *NCTE Annual Conference, Wisconsin 1968*.
— (1969), "Orthography in reading materials for black English speaking children", in: Baratz and Shuy (eds.), 1969.
Fasold, R. W. and Shuy, R. W. (eds.), (1970), *Teaching Standard English in the Inner City*. Washington, D.C., Center for Applied Linguistics.
Ferguson, G. (1954), "On learning and human ability", *Canadian Journal of Psychology* 8:95–112.
Figueroa, J. (1962), "Language Teaching: Part of a general and professional problem", *English Language Teaching* 16 (3).
— (1966), "Notes on the teaching of English in the West Indies", *New World Quarterly* 2 (4).
— (1972), "Some notes, together with samples of language occurring in the creole context", in: Craig (ed.), forthcoming.
Fishman, J. A., and Lueders-Salmon, E. (1972), "What has the sociology of language to say to the teacher? On teaching the standard variety to speakers of dialectal or sociolectal varieties", in: Cazden, John, and Hymes (eds.), 1972.
Floud, J., and Halsey, A. H. (1957), "Social class, intelligence tests and selection for secondary schools", in: Halsey, Floud, and Andefson (1961): 209–15.
Fries, C. C. (1922), *The Structure of English*. London, Longmans, Green, and Co.
— (1940), "American English grammar", *English Monograph 10*. Champaign, Illinois, NCTE.
Gaidoz, H. (1881), "Bibliographie Créole", *Revue Critique d'Histoire et de littérature*, 13 (35 and 45).
Goodnow, J. J. (1968), "Cultural variations in cognitive skills", in: Price-Williams (ed.), 1969.
Grant, D. R. B. (1964), "A study of some common language and spelling errors of elementary school children in Jamaica", in: Faculty of Education 1965.
Gray, C. (1963), "Teaching English in the West Indies", *Caribbean Quarterly*, 9 (1 and 2).
Gumperz, J., and Hymes, D. (eds.), (1972), *Directions in Sociolinguistics: The Ethnography of Communication*. New York, Holt, Rinehart & Winston.
Hall, R. (1966), *Pidgin and Creole Languages*. Ithaca, N.Y., Cornell University Press.
Hawkins, R. R. (1969), "Social class, the nominal group and reference", *Language and Speech*, 12, part 2:125–35.

Hughes, A. (1966), "Non-standard English of Grenada", *Carribbean Quarterly* 12 (4).

Hymes, D. H. (1961a), "Linguistic aspects of cross cultural personality study", in: *Studying Personality Cross Culturally*, ed. by Bert Kaplan. New York, Harper & Row.

— (1961b), "Functions of speech: An evolutionary approach", pp. 55–83 in: *Anthropology and Education*, ed. by Fred Gruber, Philadelphia, University of Pennsylvania Press.

— (1962), "The Ethnography of speaking", in: *Anthropology and Human Behaviour*, ed. by T. Gladwin and W. C. Stuyvesant. Washington, D. C., Anthropological Society of Washington.

Hymes, D. H. (ed.) (1971), *Pidginization and Creolization of Language*. Cambridge University Press.

Innis, L. O. (1910), *Trinidad and Trinidadians*. Trinidad, Mirror Printing Works.

— (1923), *Creole Folklore and Popular Superstitions in Trinidad*. Trinidad, Yuilles Printerie.

Jensen, A. R. *et al.* (1969), *Environment, Heredity and Intelligence*. Harvard Reprint, Series No 2, 1969.

John, V. P. (1962), "The intellectual development of slum children", *American Orthopsychiatric Association Annual Meeting* 1962.

Jones, J. A. (1966), "English in the West Indies", *English Language Teaching* 20 (2).

Kandel Subcommittee (1946), *Report of the Secondary Education Continuation Committee*. Jamaica, Government Printery.

Klein, J. (1965), *Samples from English Cultures*. London, Routledge and Kegan Paul.

Knight, H. E., Carrington, L. D., and Borely, C. B. (1972), *Preliminary Comments on Language Arts Textbooks in Use in the Primary Schools of Trinidad and Tobago*. U.W.I., Institute of Education.

Kochman, T. (1969), "Social factors in the consideration of teaching standard English", in Aarons and Stewart (eds.), 1969.

Labov, W. (1964), "Stages in the acquisition of standard English", in: *Social Dialects and Language Learning*, ed. by Shuy. Champaign, Illinois, NCTE.

— (1966), *The Social Stratification of English in New York City*. Washington D.C., Center for Applied Linguistics.

— (1969), *The Logic of Non-Standard English, Twentieth Annual Round Table Meeting*, No. 22, ed. by J. E. Alatis. Georgetown University School of Languages and Linguistics.

— (1971), "The notion of 'system'", in: *Creole Languages*, ed. by Hymes.

Labov, W., and Cohen, P. (1967), "Systematic relation of Standard and non-Standard rules in the grammar of negro speakers", *Project Litacy Report, 8*. Ithaca, New York, Cornell University.

Labov, W. *et al.* (1965), "A preliminary study of the structure of English used by Negro and Puerto Rican speakers in New York City", *Co-operative Research Project No. 3091*, Mimeographed report. Columbia University.

Latrobe, C. J. (1837/38), Reports on negro education, to Lord Glenelg, Secretary of State For Education and for War. Government of Great Britain.

Lawton, D. L. (1963), "Suprasegmental phenomena in Jamaica creole". Ph.D. dissertation. Michigan State University.

— (1965), "Some problems of teaching a creolized language to Peace Corps Members", *Language Learning* 14.

— (1971), "Tone and Jamaican Creole", Paper read at the Annual Conference on Caribbean Linguistics, May 17–21, Mona. Mimeo. U.W.I.

Lawton, D. (1963), "Social class differences in language development", *Language and Speech* 6 (3):120–43.

— (1964), "Social class language differences in group discussions", *Language and Speech* 7 (3):182.

— (1968), *Social Class, Language and Education*. London, Routledge and Kegan Paul.
LePage, R. B. (1952), "A survey of dialects in the British Caribbean", *Carribbean Quarterly*, 2 (3).
— (1955), "The Language problem in the British Caribbean", *Carribbean Quarterly* 4 (1).
— (1957), "General Outlines of English Creole Dialects", *Orbis* 6.
LePage, R. B. (ed.) (1961), *Proceedings of the Conference on Creole Language Studies, 1961*. London, Macmillan.
— (1972), "The concept of competence in a creole English situation", in Craig, (ed.), forthcoming.
LePage, R., and DeCamp, David (1960), *Jamaican Creole: An Historical Introduction to Jamaican Creole by R. B. LePage and Four Jamaican Creole Texts, by David DeCamp*. London, Macmillan.
Lieberson, S. (ed.) (1966), "Explorations in sociolinguistcs", *Social Enquiry* 36.
L.S.A. Bulletin (1972), *Linguistic Society of America Bulletin*, March.
Loban, W. (1963), "The language of elementary school children", NCTE, Research Report No. 1.
Long, Edward (1774), *The History of Jamaica*. Great Britain.
Luria, A. R., and Yudovich, I. (1959), *Speech and the Development of Mental Processes in the Child*. London, Staples Press.
Luria, A. R. (1961), *The Role of Speech in the Regulation of Normal and Abnormal Behaviour*. London and New York, Pergamon Press.
McClelland, C. L. *et al.* (1953), *The Achievement Motive*. New York, Appelton-Century-Crofts.
— (1958), *Talent and Society: New Perspectives in the Identification of Talent*. Princeton, New Jersey, Van Nostrand.
McClelland, D. C. (1961), *The Achieving Society*. Princeton, New Jersey, Van Nostrand.
Malinowsky, B. (1923), "The problem of meaning in primitive cultures", in: *The Meaning of Meaning*, by C. K. Ogden and I. A. Richards. London, Routledge and Kegan Paul.
Nisbet, J. (1953), "Family environment and intelligence", in: Halsey, Floud, and Anderson (1961): 273–287.
Norwood Committee (1943), *Curriculum and Examinations in Secondary Schools*. H.M.S.O.
Reissman, F. (1962), *The Culturally Deprived Child*. New York, Harper and Row.
Reisman, Karl (1961), "The English-based creole of Antigua", (Research Notes), *Caribbean Quarterly* 1 (1).
— (1965), "The isle is full of noises: A study of creole in the speech pattern of Antigua, West Indies". Ph.D. dissertation. Harvard University.
Rice, F. A. (ed.) (1962), *Study of the Role of Second Languages in Asia, Africa, and Latin America*. Washington, D.C., Center for Applied Linguistics.
Robinson, W. P. (1965), "The elaborated code in working class language", *Language and Speech* 8, Part 4, Oct.–Dec., 1965:243–52.
Robinson, W. P., and Creed, C. D. (1968), "Perceptual and verbal discriminations of 'elaborated' and 'restricted' code users", *Language and Speech* 11 (3):182–93.
Russell, T. (1868), *The Etymology of Jamaica Grammar by a Young Gentleman*. Kingston, MacDougall & Co.
Saporta, Sol, (ed.) (1961), *Psycholinguistics*. New York, Holt, Rinehart & Winston.
Schaedel, R. (ed.) (1969), *Research and Resources of Haiti*. New York, Research Institute for the Study of Man.
Schudardt, H. (1882), *Kreolisch Studien*, 11 vols. Vienna.
Scoles, I. (1885), *Sketches of African and Indian Life in British Guiana*. Guiana, The Argosy Press.

Searle, J. B. (1969), *Speech Acts: An Essay in the Philosophy of Language*. Cambridge University Press.

Shuy, R. W. (1972), "Strategies for implementing sociolinguistic principles in the schools", in: Craig (ed.), forthcoming.

Shuy, R. W. (ed.) (1964), *Social dialects and Language Learning*. Champaign, Illinois, NCTE.

— (1972), *Proceedings of the 23rd Annual Round Table*. Washington D.C., Georgetown University.

Shuy, R. W., Wolfram, W. A., and Riley, W. K. (1967), "Linguistic correlates of social stratification", in: *Detroit Speech*, Final Report. Co-operative Research Project 6-1347. Office of Education.

Solomon, D. (1966), "The system of predication in the speech of Trinidad: a quantitative study of decreolization". M.A. Thesis. Columbia University.

— (1972), "Form, content and the post-creole continuum", in: Craig (ed.). 1974.

Spears, R. (1972), "Pitch and intonation in Cayman English", in: Craig (ed.), forthcoming.

Stewart, W. A. (1962), "Creole languages in the caribbean", in: Rice (ed., 1962).

— (1967), "Sociolinguistic factors in the history of American negro dialects", *The Florida FL Reporter* 5 (2).

— (1969), "Negro dialect in the teaching of reading", in: Baratz and Shuy (eds.), 1969.

Stewart, W. A. (ed.) (1964), *Non-Standard Speech and the Teaching of English*. Washington, D.C., Center for Applied Linguistics.

Taylor, D. (1945), "Certain Carib morphological influences on creole", *International Journal of American Linguistics* 11 (3).

— (1952), "A note on the phoneme /r/ in Dominican creole", *Word* 8 (3).

— (1955), "Phonic Interference in Dominican Creole", *Word* 11.

— (1961), "Some Dominican creole descendants of the French definite article", in: *Conference on Creole Language Studies*, ed. by LePage. London, Macmillan.

— (1963), "Remarks on the lexiçon of Dominican French creole", *Romance Philology* 16.

— (1968), "New languages for old in the West Indies", in: *Readings in the Sociology of Language*, ed. by J. A. Fishman. The Hague, Mouton.

Thomas, J. J. (1869), *The Theory and Practice of Creole Grammar*. (Reprinted London, New Beacon Books. 1969.)

Trotman, J. (1973), "The teaching of English in Guyana: A linguistic approach". Mimeo. Faculty of Education, University of Guyana.

Tyndall, B. (1965), "Some grammatical aspects of the written work of creolese-speaking school children in British Guiana". M.A. thesis. University of Manchester.

— (1973), "Reading habit and the written expression of secondary school first formers". Mimeo. Faculty of Education, University of Guyana.

UNESCO (1953), "The use of vernacular languages in education: monorgaphs on fundamental education". Paris.

Valdman, A. (1969), "The language situation in Haiti", in: Schaedel (ed.), 1969.

van Name, A. (1870), "Contributions to Creole grammar", *Transactions of the American Philological Association*, 1. Boston.

van Sertima, J. (1897), "Among the common people of British Guiana", *British Guiana Pamphlet*, No. 35.

— (1905), *The Creole Tongues of British Guiana*. Berbice, British Guiana, The British Gazette Store.

Vernon. P. E. (1955), "The bearing of recent advances in psychology on educational problems", *Studies in Education* 7. University of London, Institute of Education.

— (1965a), "Environmental handicaps and intellectual development", *British Journal of Educational Psychology*, Vol. 35:1–12; 117–26.

– (1965b), "Ability factors and environmental influences", *American Psychologist* 20:723–33.
— (1966), "Education and Intellectual development among Canadian Indians and Eskimos", *Educational Review* 18:79–91; 186–95.
— (1967), "Abilities and educational attainments in an East African environment", in: Price-Williams (ed.).
Walters, E. (1958), "Learning to read in Jamaica". Mona, Jamaica, U.W.I., Department of Education.
Warner, M. (1967), "Language in Trinidad with special reference to English". M.A. thesis, University of York.
Westmaas, D. A. (1948), "On writing creolese" *Kyk-Over-All*, 2 (7), Guyana. "Some more aspects of creolese" *Kyk-Over-All*, 5 Guyana.
Wilson, E. (1968), "Grammar in English teaching", *The Guiana Teacher*, 2 (7).
Winford, D. (1972), "A sociolinguistic description of two communities in Trinidad". Ph.D. thesis. University of York.
Wolfram, W. (1969), *A Sociolinguistic Description of Detriot Negro Speech*. Washington, D.C., Center For Applied Linguistics.
— (1970), "Sociolinguistic alternatives in teaching reading to non-standard speakers", *Research Quarterly*, VI, I. Delaware.

BOOKS AND JOURNALS RECEIVED*

Alatis, James E., and Kristie Twaddell (eds.), *English as a Second Language in Bilingual Education: Selected TESOL Papers.* Washington, TESOL, 1976.

Bar-Adon, Aaron, *The Rise and Decline of a Dialect: A Study in the Revival of Modern Hebrew.* The Hague, Mouton, 1975.

Bender, M. L., J. D. Bowen, R. L. Cooper, and C. A. Ferguson, *Language in Ethiopia.* New York, Oxford University Press, 1976.

Bloch, Maurice (ed.), *Political Language and Oratory in Traditional Society.* New York, Academic Press, 1975.

Born, Warren C. (ed.), *Language and Culture: Heritage and Horizons* (= Reports of the Working Committees, Northeast Conference on the Teaching of Foreign Languages). Middlebury (Vermont), Northeast Conference on the Teaching of Foreign Languages, Inc., 1976.

Brislin, Richard W., and Paul Pedersen, *Cross-Cultural Orientation Programs.* New York, Halsted, 1976.

Clyne, Michael, *Forschungsbericht SprachKontact.* Kronberg, Scriptor, 1975.

Davies, Alan (ed.), *Problems of Language Learning.* London, Heinemann, 1975.

Depres, Leo A. (ed.), *Ethnicity and Resource Competition in Plural Societies.* The Hague, Mouton, 1975.

de Vos, George, and Lola Romanucci-Ross (eds.), *Ethnic Identity: Cultural Continuities and Change.* Palo Alto, Mayfield, 1975.

Esslinger, Dean R., *Immigrants and the City: Ethnicity and Mobility in a Nineteenth Century Midwestern City.* Port Washington (N.Y.), Kennikat Press, 1975.

Goffman, Erving, *Frame Analysis: An Essay on the Organization of Experience.* Cambridge, Harvard University Press, 1974.

— "Replies and Responses", *Working Papers and Prepublications.* (Centro Internazionale di Semiotica e di Linguistica), 1975, nos. 46–47c.

Grittner, Frank M. (ed.), *Careers, Communication and Culture in Foreign Language Teaching: A Guide for Building the Modern Curriculum* (= Report of Central States Conference on Foreign Language Education). Skokie (Ill.), National Textbook Co., 1975.

Haupenthal, Reinhard (ed.), *Plansprachen: Beitrage zur Interlinguistik.* (= Band 325, Wege der Forschung). Darmstadt, Wissenschaftliche Buchgesellschaft, 1976.

Heye, Jurgen B., *A Sociolinguistic Investigation of Multilingualism in the Canton of Ticino Switzerland.* The Hague, Mouton, 1975.

Howell, Richard W., and Harold J. Vetter, *Language in Behavior.* New York, Human Sciences Press, 1976.

Hymes, Dell, *Studies in the History of Linguistics: Traditions and Paradigms.* Bloomington (Indiana), 1974.

Jarvis, Gilbert A. (ed.), *Perspective: A New Freedom* (= ACTFL Review of Foreign Language Education #7). Skokie (Ill.), National Textbook Co., 1975.

Jermudd, Bjorn H., and Gary L. Garrison (compilers), *Language Treatment in Egypt.* Cairo (No publisher indicated, n.d. 1976?), Mimeographed.

Kalinowski, Georges, "Du métalangage en logique. Réflexion sur la logique de'ontique et son rapport avec la logiques des normes", *Working Papers and Prepublications.* (Centro Internazionale di Semiotica e di Linguistica), 1975, 48A.

* Publishers, authors and editors are requested to send all items for listing and review c/o the General Editor.

Krippner, Stanley, and Daniel Rubin, *The Energies of Consciousness*. London, Gordon and Breach, 1975.

Lafayette, Robert C. (ed.), *The Cultural Revolution in Foreign Language Teaching: A Guide for Building the Modern Curriculum* (= Report of Central States Conference on Foreign Language Education). Skokie (Ill.), National Textbook Co., 1975.

Lenneberg, Eric H., and Elizabeth Lenneberg (eds.), *Foundations of Language Development: A Multidisciplinary Approach*. 2 volumes. New York, Academic Press, 1975.

Lindekens, Rene, "Semiotique du discours publicitaire", *Working Papers and Prepublications*. (Centro Internazionale di Semiotica e di Linguistica), 1975, 45B.

Litterature Orale Arabo-Berbere, 1973–74, no. 6–7.

Luebke, Frederick C., *Bonds of Loyalty: German Americans and World War I*. DeKalb (Ill.), Northern Illinois University Press, 1974.

Reinharz, Jehuda, *Fatherland or Promised Land: The Dilemma of the German Jew, 1893–1914*. Ann Arbor, University of Michigan Press, 1975.

Rossi-Landi, Ferruccio, *Charles Morris e la Semiotica Novecentesca*. Milano, Feltrinelli, 1975.

Safa, Helen I., and Brian M. du Toit (eds.), *Migration and Development*. The Hague, Mouton, 1975.

Seelye, H. Ned, *Teaching Culture: Strategies for Foreign Language Educators*. Skokie (Ill.), National Textbook Co., 1976.

Swingwood, Alan, *Marx and Modern Social Theory*. London, Macmillan, 1975.

Thompson, Kenneth, *Auguste Comte: The Foundation of Sociology*. New York, Halstead, 1975.

Williams, Thomas R., *Socialization and Communication in Primary Groups*. The Hague, Mouton, 1975.

Working Papers on Bilingualism, 1975, no. 6.

Working Papers on Bilingualism, 1975, no. 7.

Working Papers on Bilingualism, 1976, no. 8.